Shaykh Abdul Qādir Jilāni
Life and Teachings

Ahsan Academy of Research
(Springs, South Africa)

Shaykh Abdul Qādir Jilāni
Life and Teachings

Abdul Kader Choughley

Tawasul International
Centre for Publishing, Research and Dialogue

First Published 2023
ISBN : 978-93-91601-98-0

Abdul Kader Choughley

Ahsan Academy of Research
(Springs, South Africa)
ahsan@worldonline.co.za

SHELVCRAFT™
Shelving | Racking | Display | Shop Fitting
Ph: 012 666 8933
Email: sales@shelvcraft.com
Website: www.shelvcraft.com

Published by
Tawasul International
Centre for Publishing, Research and Dialogue, Rome, Italy

CONTENTS

Acknowledgement

It is almost a decade since Anver Essa and I started the ambitious project of publishing works on the two influential Islamic scholars of the twentieth century: Dr Mawlānā Muhammad Fazlur Rahman Ansari (d.1974) and Mawlānā Abdul Aleem Siddiqui (d. 1954). Both of these illustrious *'ulama* represented the Islamic reformist thought that made impactful contributions in terms of redefining the concept of integrated Islamic knowledge in a world fractured by nationalism, secularism and materialism.

Our humble efforts have seen important publications on the life and thought of Dr Ansari and Mawlānā Siddiqui. In this perspective, *Fazlur Rahman Ansari: Aligarh Years* is a substantive work that has been recognised for its originality and meticulous research by Aligarh Muslim University (India). Likewise, *Abdul Aleem Siddiqui: Man and His Mission* is a detailed account of the Roving Ambassador of Islam's *tabligh* vision and mission in a socio-political context. The impressive reviews of these works in the widely-acclaimed Islamic journals are a testament to the scholarly contributions of these *ulama*-activists. An important work relating to the lecture series of Dr Ansari is being planned in 2023, Inshallah.

This year we have embarked on a study of the illustrious scholar-saint and reformer, Shaykh Abdul Qādir Jilāni (hereafter referred to as the Shaykh) whose immense contributions to the *tasawwuf* tradition are global in significance. Our motivation to this study is two-fold: to offer a useful guide to the life and teachings of the Shaykh and to draw instructive lessons from his celebrated works. It has been a challenging task to approach the multifaceted personality of the Shaykh in the light of his enduring legacy. Nevertheless, our study is aimed at bringing into sharp focus his life-enriching teachings in a circumstantial setting.

Allah has blessed us with this opportunity to sharing refreshing perspectives of this sublime soul whose very name evokes admiration, reverence and spontaneous prayer.

This work is dedicated to Anver for his profound love and reverence to the Shaykh. In the true spirit of promoting Islamic scholarship, it is envisaged to have a worldwide reach for scholars, professionals, Islamic institutions, libraries and readers who wish to know about the Shaykh and his contributions to Islamic reform and revival.

Abdul Kader Choughley
(Springs, South Africa)
30 January 2023

Shaykh Abdul Qādir Jilāni: Honorific Titles

To those who are familiar with the religious and spiritual legacy of Islam, there is a rich repository of honorific names and titles affixed to the luminaries of Islam. In the case of Shaykh Abdul Qādir Jilāni (hereafter the Shaykh) his followers and admirers have conferred upon him titles that are indicative of his rank and status within the *tasawwuf* tradition. In our study these dimensions are given context to understand his outstanding role as a scholar, sufi and reformer. It would be no exaggeration to state that the Shaykh enjoys this pre-eminent position which is uniquely associated to his remarkable personality.

Shaykh: A term applied throughout the Islamic world to respected persons of recognised seniority in Islamic learning, expertise, wisdom and experience. It can also refer to a spiritual guide (*murshid*) in *tasawwuf.*

'Abd al-Qādir: This is the Shaykh's personal name, meaning "Servant or Slave of the All-Powerful." There are variant spellings used in English and these appear quite frequently in this study. It is a common practice in the Muslim community to give a male child a name in which *'Abd* is prefixed to one of the Names and Attributes of Allah (*asmā' al-husnā*).

Al-Jilāni: It is a surname of the Shaykh to indicate his place of birth. He was born in the Iranian district of Gīlān, south of the Caspian Sea in 470H corresponding to 1077-8.

Sayyidundā al-Shaykh: Our Master, the Shaykh. A devoted follower of the Shaykh will generally refer to him as *Sayyidunā.*

Muhyi al-Dīn: "Reviver of the Religion." It is widely acknowledged that the Shaykh played a pioneering role in reaffirming the traditional teachings of Islam in an era when rationalistic tendencies and sectarianism sought to undermine the rich repository of its heritage and culture.

Abu Muhammad: "Father of Muhammad." In the Arabic terminology, a man's surname usually includes the name of his first-born son, with the prefix *Abu* (Father of...).

Radiya 'Allah Anh: "May Allah be pleased with him." This form of blessing is uttered for the Companions (*Sahdbah*) of the Holy Prophet (pbuh). The preference for this invocation is yet another mark of the extraordinary status held by the Shaykh in the eyes of his followers.

Al-Ghawth al-'Azam: "The Supreme Helper." *Ghawth* is an Arabic word which means: 1. A cry for aid or relief from adversity. 2. The chief of the saints (*awliyā*), who is empowered by Allah to bring relief to suffering humanity, in response to their cry for help in times of extreme adversity.

Sultān al-Awliyā: "The Sultan of the Saints." This title underscores the supremacy of the Shaykh above all other *awliyā*.

Hasani and *Husayni*: The Shaykh's noble father, 'Abdullah traced his lineage to Imam Hasan while his virtuous mother, Umm al-Khayr, traced hers to Imam Husayn, grandsons of the Holy Prophet (pbuh).

Al-Bāz al-Ashhab: "The Grey Falcon." This title is also used to describe the Shaykh's singular qualities.

In the study there is no uniform transliteration for names and places as the authors have preferred their own system. This variation is retained in the text.

Preface

In recent years there have been significant attempts to examine the extraordinary life and teachings of Shaykh Abdul Qadir al- Jilāni (hereafter the Shaykh). The widespread phenomenon of his spiritual order (*tarīqah*) and the circumstances and reasons that have given him a unique place above the rest of the sufi and saintly personalities have been researched and debated in the Western academia.[1] More importantly, the formation of the Qādiriyyah order in Baghdad and its geographical spread from the thirteenth century to modern times was a remarkable development that inspired millions of people to realign their lives according to the Qur'an and the *Sunnah* of the Holy Prophet (pbuh). In a *tasawwuf* perspective, this vision strengthened the *shari'ah-tarīqah* amalgam in an institutional form.

It is generally assumed that the Shaykh advocated *zuhd* (self-abstinence) as a panacea for the ills afflicting the Muslim society. However, the Shaykh offered a holistic approach that living apart from the mainstream society did not produce salutary outcomes. Instead, he tempered self- abstinence with positivity – a fusion of Islamic ideals that took into account the need to develop *taqwā*[2] in the Muslim collective life and experience. This point is important to understand the worldview of the Shaykh about renouncing worldly possessions for the aspirant(*murīds*)[3] who chose to achieve the highest spiritual levels as discussed in his major writings. The centrality of *taqwā* is in line with the Qur'anic emphasis on earning Allah's pleasure at all times and in all circumstances.[4]

The Shaykh lived in an era of political ferment where the Abbasid Caliphate had to contend with the rival ruling dynasties like the Seljuq

---

[1] Representative of this trend is the work of Spencer Trimingham, *The Sufi Orders in Islam* (Oxford, 1998). The Orientalist slant is discernible in the study of sufism.

[2] The term *taqwā* has various shades of meanings and can refer to fear, Allah-awareness, etc. depending on its contextual usage.

[3] The *murīd* is the seeker of Reality (*haqīqat*), who is under the mentorship of a spiritual guide (*murshid*).

[4] For a detailed discussion of the Shaykh's elaboration of leading a centred life, see Hamza Malik, *The Grey Falcon: The Life and Teaching of Shaykh 'Abd al-Qadir al-Jilāni* (Leiden, 2018), 170-83.

empire and the conflict had a direct impact on the Muslim society. As a result, there was also a proliferation of rival religious sects and militant movements that eroded the authentic teachings of the *shari'ah*. During this period, the sufi movement expanded and flourished as a representation of the mystical dimension of Islam. Against this background there was a need to harmonise *tasawwuf*[5] within the ambit of the *shari'ah*. It was the Shaykh who adopted this approach for a greater cause - service to humanity. In a particular sense the Shaykh awakened the dormant spirit of the Muslim society by restoring their faith in the abiding message of the Qur'an and the *Sunnah*. The Shaykh possessed a charismatic and eloquent personality, and had that ability to liberate the masses from their preoccupation with life's materialism.[6] Likewise, his thorough grounding in the Islamic disciplines together with his strict adherence to the *shari'ah* gave him the edge to bridge the gulf between the *faqih* (jurist) and the sufi, thus creating a balance regarding the spirit and letter of the Islamic teachings.

Teaching and preaching, to coin a phrase, dominated the Shaykh's extensive career. The multipurpose complex consisted of a public space dedicated to teaching, a *ribāt*[7] for nurturing his *murīds* (disciples) and his private apartment. We need to keep in mind that from humble beginnings the complex was expanded to accommodate the throngs of listeners to his discourses. His discourses were built around the key themes: *tawhīd* (Oneness of Allah), adherence to the *shari'ah*, leading a *taqwā*-centred life, creating a spiritual culture of Islam, and service to humanity. These have resonance in the major writings of the Shaykh and find fuller expression in the moral, ethical and spiritual ethos he advocated for the Muslim society at large.

The Shaykh was not a prolific writer in comparison to the widely-acclaimed works of Rumi (d. 1273)[8] and Ibn 'Arabi (1240).[9] These

---

[5] Generally, *tasawwuf* is associated with sufism which represents the inner dimensions of Islam. Therefore, we have used sufi(s) in the text.

[6] *Ibid.*, 216-220.

[7] *Ribāt* is synonymous with *khanqah* and is used to describe a space for performing a litany of rituals and practices under a spiritual guide (*murshid*/ *shaykh*).

[8] The multivolume *Mathnawi* is the popular work of Rumi which has been translated into major languages of the world.

[9] *Futuhāt al-Makkiya* (The Meccan Revelations) is the major work of the scholar

luminaries have attracted scholarly interest in the Western academia for various reasons and motivations. In contrast, Western writings on the Shaykh (albeit brief and limited) tend to be polemical and raise controversial issues on his charismatic personality and historical accounts, such as his miracles. In fact, there are no critical assessments of the Shaykh's celebrated works by Western scholars in terms of his contributions to *tasawwuf* or mystical dimensions of Islam[10] as this term is commonly used in their writings. As much as there are sketchy details about the Shaykh's early life and his prolonged period of spiritual wanderings (*khalawāt*),[11] no serious study has been undertaken to examine critically his *tajdidi* (revivalist) efforts to restore the primacy of the *shari'ah* within the *tasawwuf* framework.

Another lacuna to the scholarly treatment of the Shaykh's life and teachings is the embellished accounts related to his charismatic personality. Myth is conflated with reality while exaggeration is treated as absolute truth. Again, incredulous stories are woven around his extraordinary life that an almost infallible status is invested to him. Across the spectrum of incredulity is the anti-*tasawwuf* group that dismisses miracles (*karāmāt*) and *wilāyat* (friendship with Allah)[12] attributed to the Shaykh altogether. Their line of argument is rooted in their belief that *tasawwuf* is a reprehensible act (*bid'ah*)[13] and outside of the Islamic authenticity (*asliyyah*). These conflicting responses have cast a dark shadow over the true contents of faith as elaborated by the Shaykh. Needless to say, the ideological battle continues to this day.

---

and sufi, Ibn 'Arabi.

[10] See Annemarie Schimmel's *Mystical Dimensions of Islam* for a comprehensive reading of this term.

[11] In the *tasawwuf* tradition *khalwah* has a broader meaning and covers aspects of solitude, spiritual retreat or spiritual wandering.

[12] In support of their interpretation of *wilāyat*, the sufis have mentioned the following Qur'anic *āyat* (verse): "Surely the friends of Allah have nothing to fear, nor shall they grieve – the ones who believe and are Allah-fearing. For them are glad tidings in this world and in the Afterlife..." (10: 62-4)

[13] The term *bid'ah* (pl. *bid'āt*) is a subject of controversy among scholars belonging to the different schools of thought. Its connotation is used in a specific sense by the Shaykh as evident in his writings.

Our approach to the life and teachings of the revered Shaykh is two-fold: first, to highlight his contributions in a circumstantial setting; second, to broaden the horizon of his spiritual legacy in the light of his Allah-endowed insight and perspective. In this respect, credible accounts of his miracles which have been verified by renowned scholars are contextualised rather than incorporated as a separate chapter of the study. This approach is meant to show that miracles performed by the Shaykh had a life-turning experience for the people concerned. It was not a random supernatural act or an extraordinary event to reveal his spiritual prowess, but a purposeful message about the status of the *awliyā* among whom the Shaykh enjoys a pre-eminent position.

Biographical Works

The biographies of the Shaykh are mainly to be found within historical works and, therefore, are not extensive in coverage on his contribution to *islāh* (reform) and *tajdid* (revival).[14] In this respect we may refer to the biographical entries of the renowned *mufassir* (commentator of the Qur'an), Ibn Kathir (d. 1373)[15] and Ibn Rajab Hanbali (d. 1393)[16] who have given us useful information about the writings of the Shaykh and a brief overview of his students who compiled the discourses. Both these scholars have a high standing in the *hadith* literature and were meticulous in evaluating the credibility of transmitters of reports (*isnād*) which were included in their respective biographies. Shamsuddin Dhahabi (d. 1348)[17] wrote prolifically on Islamic history and biographical accounts of scholars including the Shaykh, thus enriching our understanding of the latter's significant contributions to the revivalist trends. In a similar vein, the accomplished *hadith* scholar, Hāfiz ibn Hajar al-'Asqalānī (d.

---

[14] The twin concept of *islāh* and *tajdid* are a recurrent theme in the writings of the Shaykh.

[15] 'Umar ibn Kathir, *Al-Bidāya wa al-Nihāya* (Beirut, 1988).

[16] Ahmad ibn Rajab, *Tabaqāt al-Hanābila* (Beirut, 1980). The titles have been shortened to facilitate easy reading for English speaking readers.

[17] Shamsuddin Dhahabi, *Siyar A'lām al-Nubalā'*. The text relating to the Shaykh's biography was translated by D. S. Margoliouth, *Contributions to the Biography of 'Abd Al-Kadir of Jilān*, JRAS, (1907), 267-310.

1449)[18] wrote a slim volume outlining in concise form the life of the Shaykh. These scholars showed immense respect for the Shaykh, both for his intellectual and spiritual qualities. In sum, the Shaykh carved a niche among a number of notable scholars for his mastery over the Islamic disciplines and exceptional grounding in the *tasawwuf* tradition. Although the biographical details are not comprehensive, they, nevertheless, provide a reliable account on the life and teachings of the revered Shaykh.

Hagiographical Works

A hagiography is a biography of a saint or a high-ranking religious leader in an embellished form. Simply put, it is an exaggerated account of the religious figure whose status is elevated in such a way that legendary accounts about him are considered as sacred literature. Like many pioneering personalities of Islam, the biographies of the Shaykh contain miraculous and supernatural stories and incidents that have been rejected by scholars of the calibre of Ibn Rajab and Dhahabi. However, this is not to suggest that these works have no substantive value. To illustrate a point: The first of the principal works is the *Bahjat al-Asrār* of 'Ali ibn Yusuf al-Shattanawfi (d.1314).[19] He was a reputed scholar who specialised in Qur'an recitation (*qirā'ah*) and authored this work over a hundred years after the Shaykh's death. It is an extensive source of information dealing with excerpts of the Shaykh's discourses and multiple reports of the transmission chains covering his miracles. The perceptive comment of Dhahabi has relevance: "The Shaykh Nur al-Din Shattanawfi has put together a lengthy work in three volumes on his (Jilāni's) life and work, where he has produced milk and cud in equal quantities, so to say, mixing true statements with false ones, these being given on the authority of persons with no standing or worth."[20] In Dhahabi's estimation that although the book records many miracles that are

---

[18] Hāfiz ibn Hajar al-'Asqalānī, *Ghibta al-Nazir fi Tarjumat al-Shaykh Abd al-Qadir* (Beirut, 1996).

[19] 'Ali ibn Yusuf al-Shattanawfi, *Bahjat al-Asrār* (Beirut, 1999).

[20] Cited in Malik, *The Grey Falcon*, 15.

verifiably sound, there are others that are false and narrated by unverifiable persons. Based on this evaluation by Dhahabi and other renowned scholars, *Bahjat al-Asrār* has been used with caution.

Another work that has become widely popular and used as a standard reference work is *Qalā'id al-Jawdhir* by Muhammad ibn Yahya al-Tadifi (1555).[21] It has a section on the Shaykh's attributes as well as his miracles. Likewise, he devotes a lengthy section on the sayings of the Shaykh to different topics, which are largely gleaned from the Shaykh's writings. The sons and grandsons of the Shaykh are given prominence in this work together with saints and scholars who have over the centuries commented upon the Shaykh. There is no huge gap in the timeline and we may safely assume that these sections offer significant insights into the life and times of the Shaykh.

Mulla 'Ali Qāri (d. 1605), the famous *hadith* scholar and accomplished 'alim of Hanafi fiqh authored *Nuzhat al-Khawātir al-Fātir*, a compilation of the life and teachings of the Shaykh. Although it is a concise work it lacks originality and is largely a repetition of earlier writings belonging to the hagiographical genre.

In recent years works written in Arabic and particularly in Iraq have critically examined the classical works devoted to the life and work of the Shaykh. The focus of these works covers a closer study of the writings of the Shaykh by employing critical scientific tools of the Western academia. It is heartening to note that the Qādiriyyah order and its impact worldwide has seen scholarly treatment by modern scholars analysing the phenomenal success of this great sufi movement.[22]

There is a substantial output of literature dealing with the multifaceted contributions of the Shaykh. However, these are recycled versions of hagiographical works and concentrate on the miracles attributed to the Shaykh. The *manqabah* (veneration)[23] is a salient feature of these works and in many instances the *shari'ah* boundaries are breached in their exaggerated assessment (*ghulū*) of the *tajdidi* efforts of the Shaykh. All in all, the element of infallibility

---

[21] Muhammad ibn Yahya al-Tafidi, *Qalā'id al-Jawdhir* (Beirut, 2005).

[22] See Noorah Gailani, *The Shrine of 'Abd al-Qādir al-Jilāni* (2016), 50-1.

[23] The *manqabah* genre is an integral aspect to the veneration of the *mashd'ikh* and *awliyā*. It includes poems in praise of these great figures of Islam.

takes centre stage with the result that the authentic teachings of the Shaykh are relegated to the margins.

A seminal work in English, *The Saint of Jilān*[24] by S.A. Salik was brought out in 1939. Apart from its mediocre style and repetition of information, it focuses on the Qādiriyyah order in the Indian subcontinent. Another work *The Sultan of the Saints*[25] by Muhammad Riaz Qadri is representative of this trend. Although detailed information is provided about the life and contributions of the Shaykh it tends to gravitate towards embellished accounts[26] that mar the merit of this important work. In addition, eulogy of the Shaykh is given disproportionate prominence.

A work of serious academic merit is *The Grey Falcon* authored by Hamza Malik. It is a pioneering piece of writing in many respects: a critical appraisal of the life and times of the Shaykh, followed by an exploration of key themes gleaned from his discourses. *Fiqh*, theology (*kalām*) and *tasawwuf* are organically analysed to bring out the significance of the Shaykh's teachings and his lasting legacy. Another important work dealing with the sufi orders or brotherhood is *Muslim Communities of Grace* [27] by Jamil Abun-Nasr. This comprehensive and illuminating book traces the evolution of the sufi brotherhoods and their quest for legitimacy within the *shari'ah-tarīqah* framework. It also gives a fascinating account about the phenomena of the tarīqahs and how they operated without state interference, enjoying their own religious autonomy. For our study, the section on the Shaykh makes interesting reading. Abun-Nasr also draws upon important sources to point out the factors that led to the expansion of the Qādiriyyah order. Of interest also are the contributions of the Shaykh's son, 'Abdur Razzāq who played a pivotal role in giving shape to the *shari'ah-tarīqah* amalgam and com-

---

[24] Saiyed Abdus Salik, *The Saint of Jilān* (Calcutta, 1939).

[25] Muhammad Riaz Qadri, *The Sultan of the Saints: Mystical Life and Teachings of Hazrat Shaikh Syed Abdul Qādir Jilāni* (New Delhi, 2020).

[26] Embellished accounts cover exaggeration (*ghulū*) and fabricated stories which blur the authentic presentation of eminent scholar-sufis like the Shaykh. The multiple titles prefixed to their names are another blemish in their biographies.

[27] Jamil Abun Nasr, *Muslim Communities of Grace* (London, 2007).

piling the utterances and discourses of his noble father.[28]

Literary Works of the Shaykh

A list of twenty-five titles has been attributed to the Shaykh; however, many of these works have been compiled bearing his name. For our study purpose, the following books have been utilised in our examination of the essential teachings of the Shaykh. Muhtar Holland (d. 2010) is to be credited for translating the major writings of the Shaykh – a splendid accomplishment for readers interested in the multifaceted contributions of this great scholar-sufi.

Al-Ghunya li-Tālibi is a handbook or ethico-legal manual[29] written for Sunni Muslims describing the moral, ethical and social duties to be practised by the Muslim believer. It is also divided into several sections that deal with matters of *fiqh* (jurisprudence) and the tenets of faith (*'aqidah*). The book concludes with a short account of *tasawwuf.* The motivation for composing this book is described by the Shaykh in these words: "One of my friends had been pressing me, urging me in very emphatic terms to compose this book, because of his excellent appreciation of what is right and proper... I came to recognise the sincerity of his wish to acquire real knowledge of modes of behaviour consistent with the sacred law (*shari'ah*)..., real knowledge of the Maker (Almighty the Glorious is He)., instruction in the Qur'an and the *Sunnah*, and real knowledge of the morals and ethics of the righteous. All of these subjects we shall review in the course of the book, so that it may serve as an aid to him in following the path of Allah, in carrying out His commandments and observing His prohibitions."[30]

Al-Fath ar-Rabbāni is a collection of sixty-two discourses delivered by the Shaykh in the years 545-6H/1150-1152. Muhtar Holland, in his translation of the book, quotes D. S. Margoliouth's evaluation of this inspirational work: "The sermons (discourses) included in [this

---

[28] *Ibid.,* 82-6.

[29] The Shaykh formulated a clear-cut presentation of ethics within the *shari'ah* framework in his *Ghunya.*

[30] Shaikh 'Abd Al-Qādir Al-Jilāni, *Al-Ghunya li Tālibi Tariq al-Haqq: Sufficient Provision for Seekers of the Path of Truth* (Florida, 1997).

work] are some of the very best in Muslim literature, the spirit of which they breathe in one of charity and philanthropy: the preacher [the Shaykh] would like to 'close the gates of Hell and open those of Paradise to all mankind.' He employs sufi technicalities very rarely, and none of these would occasion (give) the reader much difficulty."[31]

Futuh al-Ghaib is a collection of seventy-eight *maqālāt*[32] (discourses) that were verbally delivered by the Shaykh. These were transcribed, compiled and published by his son 'Abd al- Razzaq. It is considered to be a literary work studded with the gems of *tasawwuf*; the discourses cover issues related to *'aqā'id* (Islamic beliefs and doctrines), key concepts that foster the inner dimensions of Islam, such as fear and hope; seeking to draw near to Allah; the conditions of the *nafs* (the self) and the stages of the seeker's (*murid's*) state.[33]

Jalā' al-Khawdtir is a collection of forty-five discourses by the Shaykh which were delivered during 1152. The overlapping features of this work with some of the discourses in *Fath ar- Rabbāni* lead to the assumption that it was spread over a ten- week period between 9th Rajab and 14th Ramadan 546H.[34]

Sirr al-Asrār is a collection of twenty-four sections and considered a literary piece of work on *tasawwuf*. It explores a variety of aspects dealing with the realities of faith, and the external and inner paths (*turuq*) a believer has to take to complete his journey towards Allah.[35]

Mukhtasar fi Ilm ad-Din contains two sets of chapters in which the Shaykh deals concisely with both the outer (*zāhir*) and inner (*bātin*)[36] dimensions of Islam. Included in this work is an Appendix, containing eighteen discourses named *Pearls of the Heart* – a

---

[31] Shaikh 'Abd Al-Qādir Al-Jilāni, *Al-Fath ar-Rabbāni: The Sublime Revelation* (Florida, 1992).

[32] The term *maqālāt* is interchangeably used for *mawd'iz*, both of which carry a similar import.

[33] Shaikh 'Abd Al-Qādir Al-Jilāni, *Futuh al-Ghaib: Revelations of the Unseen* (Kuala Lumpur, 1995).

[34] Shaikh 'Abd Al-Qādir Al-Jilāni, *Jalā" Al-Khawātir: The Removal of Cares* (Florida, 1997).

[35] Shaikh 'Abd Al-Qādir Al-Jilāni, *Sirr al-Asrār: The Secret of Secrets* (Cambridge, 1992). This work has been translated and interpreted by Shaykh Tosun Bayrak a-Jerrahi al-Halveti.

[36] These terms are elaborated in *Futuh al-Ghaib* and are an indicator of the Shaykh's balanced presentation of the ideals of *tasawwuf*.

summative exposition of the means to reach Allah.[37]

Fifteen Letters was originally written in Persian and translated into Arabic. These letters comprise nuggets of wisdom couched in various literary forms and capture the essence of *tasawwuf*.[38]

Malfūzāt is considered a supplement to the older versions of *Fath ar-Rabbāni* and were fragments of his utterances in his *majālis* [39] (sessions) that were eventually gathered together in a single compilation.[40]

The above listed works have been consulted in the preparation of this volume.

As mentioned elsewhere in the chapter the versatility of the Shaykh's contributions comes to the fore in respect of his *tajdidi*[41] (revivalist) efforts. His vision and mission statement were a clarion call to reinvigorate the spirit of Islam to the masses of Baghdad and beyond within the framework of the *shari'ah* and *tarīqah*. This approach is discernible in his celebrated works and can be considered a turning point in giving *tasawwuf* a viable institutional form.

The methodology adopted in the study is aimed at reconstructing the life and teachings of the Shaykh in a specific socio-political milieu. It is through his writings that we are able to understand the range of his revolutionary ideas and deep- seated concern for the amelioration of the Muslim society and humanity at large. The Shaykh strongly maintained that the loss of faith was the direct result of moral and spiritual decline and, therefore, needed a total overhaul. His discourses caught the imagination of the masses and his

---

[37] Shaikh 'Abd Al-Qādir Al-Jilāni, *Mukhtasar fi 'Ilm ad-Din: The Summary of Religious Knowledge and Pearls of the Heart* (Florida, 2010).

[38] Shaikh 'Abd *Al-Qādir Al-Jilāni, Khamsata 'Ashara Maktūbān: Fifteen Letters* (Florida, 1997).

[39] In our study *majlis* (pl. *majālis*) refers to the assembly or session that the Shaykh used to conduct for his listeners. If there was a crowded audience he would have his *majlis* in the open air.

[40] Shaikh 'Abd Al-Qādir Al-Jilāni, *Malfūzāt: Utterances* (Florida, 1992)

[41] The term *tajdid* has a broader definition in terms of its scope, function and relevance in Islamic history. As a *mujaddid* (revivalist), the Shaykh played a vital role in restating the teachings of the Qur'an and the *Sunnah* as indispensable guides for the *ummah*.

charisma renewed their commitment to lead a *taqwā*-centred life. It was elevating the soul to the divine. Overall, the Shaykh possessed a unique character and it is through the prism of his eventful life that we see him as a scholar, sufi and reformer of undisputed stature. The miraculous events attributed to the Shaykh are another feature that reinforces his peerless personality. In sum, the Shaykh continues to be a source of inspiration to the *ummah* and a succour to the ailing humanity suffering from the blight of corruption, anarchy and unbridled materialism.

It is hoped that the present volume will stimulate greater interest among scholars and academicians to undertake future studies related to the multidimensional contributions of the Shaykh who enriched Muslim history in the diverse fields he embodied in his life and teachings.

Life and Teachings of Shaykh Abdul Qādir Jilāni: A Synopsis

Shaykh's honorific title is Muhyi al-Din[1] Abu Muhammad. He was born in 470H/1077, in the province of Gilān or Jilān to the south of the Caspian Sea. He died in Baghdad in 561H/1166, at the age of ninety-one.

On his father's side the Shaykh traced his descent to the venerable Imam Hasan, grandson of our master, Allah's Messenger (Allah bless him and give him peace). Both his parents were among the renowned saints (*awliyā*) of the time.

His Education

The Shaykh acquired most of his education in Baghdad. He studied grammar, syntax and similar sciences under Imam al-Tabrizi, *hadith* under Abu Nasr Mubarak and Islamic jurisprudence (*fiqh*) under the greatest jurists at that time. Apart from his mastery of the Hanbali *fiqh*, he was especially well-versed in the jurisprudence of Imam al-Shāfi'ī[2] and also used to issue formal legal opinions (*fatāwā*) according to this school of thought.

The Shaykh learned *tasawwuf* from Abu'l Khayr al-Dabbas, the famous sufi in Baghdad, and this became his favourite subject from then on.

---

[1] Muhyi al-Din is an honorific title that describes the Shaykh's role as the reviver of religion (Islam) in an era of irreligiousness, crass materialism and political instability.

[2] There are four schools of Islamic jurisprudence: Hanafi, Shafi'i, Maliki and Hanbali.

His Characteristic Style

The Shaykh was a powerful orator, an eloquent preacher, and a sufi endowed with abstinence (*zuhd*)[3] and true devotion. As well as being an expert in the art of public speaking, the Shaykh had an excellent awareness of people's psychological condition. He would address a crowded audience with his extensive culture and knowledge, and he would leave everyone charmed and astonished. The audience he attracted became too large to be contained in the mosque or the school-house (*madrasah*), so the Shaykh was eventually compelled to lecture in the open air. He used to lecture three times a week at various places. Far from inflicting boredom on his audience, the Shaykh would everyday increase their enthusiasm and delight. Groups of people would travel great distances to attend his lecture, and on the day of his lecture, the streets of Baghdad would assume the appearance of a marketplace.

The Nature of his Knowledge

The Shaykh was an extremely erudite Islamic scholar. He was well-versed in the sciences of the *hadith, fiqh* and *tasawwuf.* He was profoundly well-informed about doctrinal matters (*'aqā'id*) and took a great interest in *tafsir* studies. The Shaykh

---

[3] Although the Shaykh practised *zuhd* (abstinence) in his personal life, it was an activist one that did not cut off ties from family and community life nor did he exhort people, more specifically his *murīds* (disciples) to renounce the world.

was in the fullest sense a perfect human being (*Insān-e Kāmil*) and this accounts for him being called 'The Grey Falcon' and the 'Sultan of the Saints'.

His Charismatic Talents (*Karāmāt*)

Many of the Shaykh's *karāmāt*[4] are discussed in several works. These reinforce his stature as a great saint (*wali*) and spiritual guide. The fact that the Shaykh caused thousands of misguided persons to follow the right path and attain right guidance is a testament to his sublime status.

The works of the Shaykh comprising a repository of illuminating discourses arc vcry beneficial to this day.[5]

---

[4] *Karāmāt* (sing. *karāmat*) are charismatic gifts or supernatural acts or miracles which Allah bestows upon the *awliyā*. These are distinguished from the miracles (*mu'jizāt*) of the Messengers of Allah.
[5] Adapted from *Pearls of the Heart*, 91-94

CHAPTER ONE

Early Life and Charismatic Personality: Political Conditions in Baghdad

No biographical study on the life and times of Shaykh Abdul Qādir Jilāni is complete without providing the historical development of Muslim rule, particularly in Baghdad.[1] The metropolis of Islamic culture and learning, the hub of Islamic *'ulum* (sciences), the epicentre of *tasawwuf* – Baghdad was the confluence of Islamic and foreign sciences under the patronage of the Abbasid rule. In fact, the early Abbasid period is regarded as an era of unique achievement. Caliphs like Harun al-Rashid and Ma'mun patronised the intellectual movements on the rise which gave impetus to the infiltration of Persian, Indian and Hellenist (Greek) thought.[2] The Persian influence, apart from its military presence, was visible in the field of art and literature, while medicine and astronomy of Indian origin made its mark on Arabic intellectual thought. However, the impact of Greek philosophy and theology had a decisive impact in the Arab world. Muslim scholars integrated these disciplines into their intellectual worldview and presented a cogent defence of the religious theories that purported to be in line with Islamic teachings.

The twelfth century saw the emergence of multiple sufi orders, which traced their spiritual lineage to great scholar-sufis like Abu Hāmid al-Ghazāli (d. 1111)[3] and Shaykh Abdul

---

[1] See Hamza Malik, *The Grey Falcon: The Life and Teaching of Shaykh 'Abd al- Qādir al-Jilāni* (Leiden, 2018), 33-65. Cf. Abul Hasan Ali Nadwi, *Saviours of Islamic Spirit*, vol. 1 (London, 2015), 163-4.

[2] *Ibid.*, 51-4.

[3] For a comprehensive study of Ghazāli's life and thought, see Mohamed Abu Bakr

Qādir Jilāni (hereafter the Shaykh). Al-Ghazāli was a pre-eminent scholar whose writings, particularly the multivolume *Ihyā 'Ulum*[4] had immortalised his fame as an influential figure who not only critiqued Greek philosophy, but also presented a well-developed understanding about the inner dimensions of Islam. His spiritual retreat is poignantly described in his autobiography.[5] An important point to be noted is the critical evaluation of Muslim writings in philosophy which tended to extol the founders of Greek thought. Ghazāli stood as a bastion against this line of thought which in many ways subjected the pristine teachings of Islam to speculative theology. Reason was given preference over revelation (*wahy*) by diluting the simple and direct message of the Qur'ān. It was, therefore, not surprising for polemical literature and 'enlightened' schools of thought to be patronised by the Caliphs of the day.

Baghdad also saw the growth and development of schools of jurisprudence (*fiqh*) among which was the influential Hanafi school founded by Imām Abu Hanifa.[6] For our study purpose, the presence of the Hanbali school in Baghdad, founded by Imam Ahmad bin Hanbal, was promoted by illustrious scholars like the Shaykh. The amalgam of *shari'ah* and *tasawwuf* was more pronounced in their *tajdidi* (revivalist) efforts to draw the *ummah* closer to the message of the Qur'ān and the *Sunnah*. The Shaykh was the embodiment of this ideal as is shown in his

---

Al-Musleh, *Al-Ghazāli: The Islamic Reformer* (Kuala Lumpur, 2012).
[4] *Ihyā 'Ulum al-Din* (Revival of the Religious Sciences) is a masterpiece of the revivalist-theme literature. It has had an enduring impact on the *tasawwuf* tradition. In recent years a complete series has been brought out in English which is illustrative of its growing popularity for readers seeking to understand the inner dimensions of Islamic thought.
[5] *Al-Munqidh min al-Dalāl* (Deliverance from Error).
[6] An excellent study on the development of *fiqh* appears in Muhammad Abu Zahra, *The Four Imams: The Lives and Teachings of their Founders* (London, 1999).

major works.

The political situation in Baghdad prior to as well as during the Shaykh's time was volatile due to the changing fortunes brought about by the Seljuq rulers. The disputes arose on the line of succession which invariably was a hereditary issue. The Seljuqs ruled over Iraq and Iran and were staunch Sunnis. Like most Turkish tribes they belonged to the Hanafi school of law. As a result, the Abbasid Caliphs were nominal rulers, almost co-opted by the Seljuq dynasty to preserve their institutional memory in the metropolis. Over time the Seljuq rulers sought to establish the *shari'ah* as the 'organising principle of the community' and, therefore, enlisted scholars from other schools of law to provide a coherent and flexible character to the Sunni state control.[7] It was Al-Ghazāli who provided the theoretical framework[8] of this new situation.

Baghdad saw the mass influx of immigrants who were ethnically composed of Arabs, Turks, Persians and Turks. There was also a sizeable Christian, Jewish and Zoroastrian population. All in all, the metropolis developed a distinct religious character and it was not uncommon that a particular school of law claimed to be the upholder of Islamic law and morality; in this case, the Hanbalis were one of the largest groups who played an active role in the city. The Shaykh was a Hanbali and contributed exceptionally to the upliftment of the Muslim community.

---

[7] Malik, *The Grey Falcon*, 42-3.
[8] Ghazāli's *Nasihat al-Muluk* (Counsels for Kings) restates the message for Muslim rulers to pattern their kingdoms (*sultanates*) along Islamic lines.

Birth and Lineage

Shaykh Abdul Qadir was born in 1077 in Gīlān,[9] a northwest province of Iran. Its political boundary with Russia is marked by the Astara stream and is one of the most beautiful areas of Iran. It is wrongly assumed that his family was of Persian origin on account of his birthplace. He was an Arab by descent, but hailed from Persia due to the migration of his ancestors. He was the tenth descendant of Imām Hasan ibn 'Ali, the son of the fourth righteous caliph of Islam.[10]

The father of the Shaykh was Abu Sālih Jangi Dost.[11] This appellation refers to his love for *jihād*. According to historical accounts he possessed a sublime soul and was devoted to *dhikr* (contemplation) and *zuhd* (austere lifestyle). These qualities were ingrained in this illustrious Hasani lineage. Always meticulous about the minutest detail regarding the sources of *halāl* his innate nature and *rūhāni* (spiritual) disposition would balk at the very thought of being involved even in condonable (*mubah*) things. The following incident is illustrative of his spiritual stature and Allah's divine plans.

Once Abu Sālih sat on the bank of a river in deep contemplation with closed eyes. When he opened his eyes, he felt very hungry, because he had not taken meals for a few days. He saw an apple floating down the stream. When it came near the bank, he took it and ate it. Immediately his conscience

---

[9] Jilān is widely used in English and Arabic works.

[10] The lineage of the Shaykh, Hasani and Husayni, is given in Muhammed Ibn Yahya At-Tadifi, *Qalā'id al-Jawāhir*, 8-9. Translated into English by Muhtar Holland as *Necklaces of Gems* (Florida, 1998). Al-Baz Publishing Inc. has been responsible for bringing out the complete works of the Shaykh in English.

[11] The title *Jangi Dost* has created a misperception that the Shaykh's family was of Persian origin. Hailing from Gilan, the people regarded Abu Sālih as one who had the passion for *jihād*, hence the Persian title.

unsettled him as he doubted whether the apple was lawful for him. He resolved to trace the source of the apple and after three days' arduous journey he saw an apple tree, a large garden and a spacious building. Likewise, he noticed some apples fall into the river which he strongly believed that the apple he had eaten had fallen from the same tree. On enquiry he was informed that the owner of the garden was Shaykh Abdullah Sawma'i, a distinguished *'alim* and shaykh of his time. Abu Sālih approached him and begged his pardon for having eaten the apple without his permission. Shaykh Sawma'i perceived the humility and nobility of Abu Sālih's character and replied that he would only forgive him if the latter agreed to be in his service for twelve years. Abu Sālih readily agreed. After twelve years Shaykh Sawma'i added another condition in these words: "I shall pardon you if you agree to marry my daughter, who is blind and deaf and whose hands are paralytic and legs are lame. In addition, you need to live with me for another two years so that I may have the pleasure of seeing a grandson." Abu Sālih agreed to the proposal and the marriage (*nikāh*) was solemnised. At night when he entered the room of the bride, he saw an extremely beautiful woman free from the physical disabilities described by her father. He lowered his gaze thinking that he had entered a wrong room. The next morning Shaykh Sawma'i who possessed intuitive insight and illuminating disclosure (*kashf*)[12] understood the dilemma faced by Abu Sālih. He explained: "I had stated that my daughter was blind, because her eyes never fell on any *ghayr mahram* (man whom she could lawfully marry according to *shari'ah*). She was deaf, because she never

---

[12] There are different categories of *kashf*, highlighting the knowledge of Reality (*haqiqat*) and also increasing the *'abd's* (servant/slave) yearning and intense love for Allah.

heard any untruthful statements and vain talks; likewise, her hands were paralytic because she never touched any *ghayr mahram*. In the same vein, she was lame because she never stepped towards any wrong acts."[13]

Abu Muhammad Abdul Qadir traced his Husayni lineage from his devout mother Fatima Umm al-Khayr, daughter of Shaykh Abdullah Sawma'i. He was one of the leading scholars in Jilān famed for his lofty spiritual states (*ahwāl)* and *karāmāt.*[14] Many of his contemporaries attested to his position as "one whose supplication was always answered." A noteworthy incident underscores his spiritual affinity and charismatic personality. A caravan was attacked by marauding horsemen in the desert of Samarqand. The helpless traders cried out to Shaykh Sawma'i who appeared in their midst. He uttered the call: "All-Glorious, All-Holy (*Subbuh Quddus*) is our Lord, Allah. Be gone from us, O you horsemen." Through Allah's help these horsemen were scattered in the mountain peaks and deep valleys protecting the traders from their potential assault. When they looked for the shaykh they could not find him. On their return to Jilān they discovered that he had never left the place.[15] This anecdote also reveals the nurturing environment in which Shaykh Abdul Qādir was raised. His father's level of *taqwā* was steeped in the *tasawwuf* tradition; his mother was a virtuous woman who exemplified the ethos of goodness (*khayr*); his maternal grandfather possessed extraordinary qualities and was the epitome of *ihsān* (moral excellence). All in all, he was endowed with spiritual grace (*fayd*) through his Hasani-

---

[13] Saiyed Abdus Salik, *The Saint of Jilan* (Delhi, 1939), 3-4.

[14] A *karāmat* is a miracle wrought by Allah through a *wali* (saint) or pious person for the good of the people. It is also a proof of his sainthood (*wilāyat*) as a miracle of divine favour.

[15] *Qalā'id al-Jawāhir*, 9.

Husayni lineage that prepared him for the pivotal role in the domain of *tajdid* (revival).

Childhood and Early Education

The Shaykh's mother relates that when she gave birth to him, he would not suck her breast during the daytime of Ramadan. The new moon of Ramadan was hidden by clouds and so the people came to her and asked about her blessed son. She replied that he had not sipped a breast today implying that it was obviously the first of Ramadan. The word went around in the towns of Jilān that a son had been born to the noble (*sharif*) couple through whose act the month of Ramadan was established.[16] This was already a sign by divine providence of the infant's spiritual stature that would be recognised not only in Baghdad, the site of his reform (*islāhi*) activities, but would also resonate centuries later all over the world.

The Shaykh received his elementary Islamic education from his grandfather Shaykh Sama'i. His father had passed away when he was a young boy and, therefore, he was raised by his mother. He completed his memorisation of the Qur'ān and learnt what he could in his hometown. Jilān contained only small villages and had limited access to higher Islamic learning. For any aspirant student Baghdad was the destination point to acquire Islamic *'ulum*[17].

We return to the Shaykh's early years in Jilān. There are several

---

[16] Ibid., 10.

[17] *'Ulum* covers the various Islamic subjects and details the intensive study programme a student had to undergo to receive the credentials of an *'alim* worthy of recognition.

anecdotes that relate to his detachment from frivolous games commonly enjoyed by boys of his age. However, there was a guiding hand, an inner voice reminding him that his calling was greater than these mundane activities. When he was ten years old students were asked in a classroom to make space for the saint- a direct reference to the Shaykh by a stranger whose whereabouts were not known. In many instances these were saintly figures (*awliyā*) heralding the greatness of people selected by Allah to devote their lives to the cause of Islam.[18] The Shaykh was uniquely endowed with this illustrious position as discussed elsewhere in the study.

Truth leads to Righteousness

The Shaykh realised that Islamic higher learning could only be sought outside Jilān and in this case it was the famous city of Baghdad. At the age of eighteen he took his mother's permission to pursue his advanced studies under the eminent scholars of his time. It was no easy decision for Fatima Umm al-Khayr to allow her beloved son to venture into a new world which entailed many challenges. In addition, Baghdad was the metropolis of Islam and unlike Jilān possessed a cosmopolitan character embodying different sectarian affiliations. Even under these circumstances she realised the irrepressible aspirations of the Shaykh to pursue Islamic knowledge tempered with *tarbiyyah*[19] (moral training). There is an anecdotal account with regard to his initial journey to Baghdad that illustrates his truthfulness and virtuous character even as a young boy.

---

[18] Muhammad Riaz Qadri, *The Sultan of Saints: Mystical Life and Teachings of Hazrat Shaikh Syed Abdul Qadir Jilani* (New Delhi, 2016), 14-5.

[19] In the context of the study *tarbiyyah* has a wider connotation and embodies moral uprightness, nurturing environment and character development.

Essentially it is a profound statement about his spiritual aura which changed the lives of irreligious people.

Before the Shaykh left his home, his mother gave him forty dinars for the journey and to get him started as a student in Baghdad. She had inherited these dinars from her father and sewed them into the lining under the armpit of his shirt for safety purpose. At the same time, she made him promise to always tell the truth under every circumstance. And with this counsel the Shaykh left Gīlān never to see his mother in person again. When she stepped out of the house to bid him farewell, she said: "O my son, away you go, for I have detached myself from you for the sake of Allah, knowing that I shall not see this (blessed) face of yours again, until the day of Resurrection (*Yawm al-Qiyāmah*)."[20]

During the journey while passing through an area called Fallat, the small caravan was ambushed by a group of around sixty bandits. These were highwaymen notorious for their sudden attacks on caravans enroute to Baghdad and its periphery. Initially, these bandits did not take notice of the Shaykh, while one of them came to him and randomly asked if he had anything in his possession. The Shaykh kept his composure and calmly replied that he had forty dinars under his armpit sewn into the cloth of his shirt. The bandit shrugged off his reply thinking that the Shaykh was being funny and left him alone. The bandits gathered on a nearby hill and divided the loot from the caravan. The bandit who had spoken with the Shaykh informed their leader about the latter's reply and thus was ordered to appear before the head of the gang. The leader asked the Shaykh what

---

[20] *Qalā'id al-Jawāhir*, 33.

he had with and again he gave the same reply that he had forty dinars sewn into the lining of his shirt, pointing specifically to the armpit area. The leader ordered the cloth to be ripped apart and found the forty dinars.[21] The following conversation reveals the effect of the Shaykh's truthfulness on the bandits:

"Whatever prompted you to make this confession?" the leader wanted to know.

So, I (the Shaykh) told him: "My mother took a promise to commit myself to truthfulness (*sidq*), and I would never betray this promise with her."

As soon as he heard these words, the leader began to weep, and he said through his tears: "You did not betray your mother's promise, whereas I have been betraying the covenant of my Lord!"

He thereupon repented at my hands, and his fellow bandits said to him: "You have been our leader in highway robbery, and now you shall be our leader in repentance (*tawba*)."

"So, they all repented at my hands, and they restored to the caravan whatever items they had seized from the travellers. They were thus, the very first of those sinners who have by now repented at my hands."[22]

Two important points emerge from this incident. First, the Shaykh was guided by the Qur'ānic teaching of *sidq* (truthfulness) which was embedded in his life as a young boy. For him speaking the truth was non-negotiable in any circumstances and no pressure or challenge would sway him from expressing boldly this principle which was intrinsic to his noble character. Second, historians report that a large segment of Baghdad's inhabitants was inspired by his discourses to repent at his hands

---

[21] Malik, *The Grey Falcon*, 77-8.
[22] *Qalā'id al-Jawāhir*, 33-4.

and thousands of Jews, Christians and people belonging to other faiths and sects were honoured to accept Islam.[23] In sum, this epoch-making incident was a precursor to the pioneering role the Shaykh was to play in later years to the reconstruction of Muslim society.

[23] Nadwi, *Saviours of Islamic Spirit*, vol. 1, 166.

Chapter Two

Education and Spiritual Training: An Assessment

Before we attempt to discuss the Shaykh's pursuit of knowledge it will be useful to reconstruct the prevalent educational system of education in Baghdad. There were three sites of learning to cater for the scholarly tradition which was firmly entrenched due to the presence of illustrious *'ulama* and the patronage of the rulers of the time.

The *jāmi'* was principally a large mosque that had the right to conduct Friday congregational prayers (*salāh*). This was in line with the Caliphal order and, therefore, we find that there were only six *jawāmi'*[1] in the eleventh century. Scholars would teach *hadith*, *fiqh* and other Islamic subjects excluding foreign sciences, such as Greek philosophy. Moreover, they were appointed by the Caliph based on the recommendations from other leading scholars. The shaykh or professor was assigned a chair as a mark of authority and he would usually hold tenure for the rest of his life. The chair that the shaykh held would either be known by the subjects he taught or by the name of the family that occupied it. This system of teaching also highlighted the academic credentials of the shaykh.[2]

The *masjid* was used for the five daily prayers in congregation (*jamā'at*) and for education. However, there was no lodging for teachers and students and often they were put up in a *khān* (inn/ lodge house) which was set up as a *waqf* (endowment), a

---

[1] These were principal mosques offering an array of Islamic subjects.
[2] See George Makdisi, *The Rise of Colleges: Institutions of Learning in Islam and the West* (Edinburgh, 1981), 12-3.

system very much in vogue in the Muslim world. Initially, the *masjids* would teach *fiqh* and *hadith* together with other ancillary subjects; however, over the course of time they would teach one of the four schools of law.[3]

The *madrasah* was a marked departure from the institutions listed above. Although law (*fiqh*) was its main focus, other subjects were also taught such as *hadith*, Arabic grammar, etc. The standard of teaching was exceptionally high as there were many shaykhs who were specialists in their respective Islamic subjects. They also held the position of a professor, a designation that indicated their standing in the scholarly community. The Nizāmiyyah was the first higher institution of learning built by the vizier Nizām al-Mulk who served as its patron and financially endowed it. As its patron he had the power to dismiss shaykhs from their teaching positions as he willed. The Nizāmiyyah[4] gained popularity on two counts: first, lodging for students was provided within its precincts; second, students enjoyed a good measure of financial stability with its scholarship scheme.[5]

In the Hanbali circle two scholars stand out for their popularity among the masses. The Jāmi' Mansur was used by Abu Yā'la for his *halaqah* after Friday prayers that three transmitters were needed to amplify his lecture to the farthest corners of the mosque.[6] Likewise, his student Abu Sa'id al-Mukharrimi (d. 1119) built a *madrasah* in the Bāb al-Azaj Quarter where he lived. It was later given to the Shaykh, his famous student at which time it was expanded and renamed as Madrasah Shaykh

---

[3] *Ibid.*, 21-22.
[4] Al-Ghazāli was the renowned professor of this institution and gained fame on account of his brilliant writings.
[5] *Ibid.*, 23-4.
[6] Malik, *The Grey Falcon*, 60.

'Abd al-Qādir.[7] (see map of Medieval Baghdad).

There are two significant phases to the Shaykh's pursuit of knowledge journey in Baghdad and are discussed in detail.

The Shaykh had left Jilān to travel to Baghdad which was famed for its centuries-long Islamic culture and civilisation. It offered a comprehensive curriculum that blended *ta'lim* with *tarbiyyah*.[8] In contrast, there were other movements and sects, such as the Mu'tazilah[9] advocating a rational interpretation of Islam, often in collision with the creed *('aqā'id)* of the *Ahl al-Sunnah wa'l Jamā'ah*. The Shaykh chose the *madrasah* of the Hanbali scholars as it was the predominant school of law and had reputed scholars who were credited for their specialisation in their respective Islamic subjects. His teachers in *tafsir* and *hadith* included Ibn 'Aqil, Muhammad ibn Hasan al-Bāqillāni, *fiqh* under Shaykh Mukharrimi and Arabic literature under the noted Abu Zakariyyah al-Tabrizi. The Shaykh is also known to have studied the Shāfi'i *fiqh* as well and was able to give legal rulings *(fatāwā)* in both Hanbali and Shafi'i schools.[10] The list of his teachers underscore his deep study and thorough grasp of these *'ulum*.[11]

The Shaykh spent his early years acquiring knowledge under extremely straitened circumstances, but starvation and penury

---

[7] *Qalā'id al-Jawāhir*, 16-7.

[8] These terms are also interchangeably used for the *shari'ah-tariqah* amalgam in the study. In fact, the thrust area of the Shaykh's revivalist efforts is based on this important aspect of Islam.

[9] For a critical evaluation of the Mu'tazilah, see M. M. Sharif, *A History of Muslim Philosophy*, vol. 1 (Karachi 1983), 199-219. The sect's deviance from the mainstream Islam is based on their extreme rationalist approach. This approach explains their rejection of the miracles *(karāmāt)* of the saints *(awliyā)*.

[10] Ibn Hajr Al-Asqalānī, *Ghibta al-Nazir*. Translated into English as *The Onlooker's Delight*, 299-301.

[11] See Muhammad Dawud Faruqi, *Sirat-i Ghaws-i 'Azam* (Amritsar, 1926), 44-5. The list includes a few scholars who taught at the famous Nizāmiyyah institution.

could not dampen his zeal and resilience. Having spent the forty dinars for his basic necessities he was exposed to the hazards of living in a metropolis like Baghdad. He could have easily been enrolled at Nizāmiyyah, which apart from promoting the Shafi'i school of law also offered a stipend for the students. In contrast, the Shaykh's *taqwā* was tested on the crucible of trials and tribulations in order to perfect his levels of spirituality. There are several incidents relating to these trials; two incidents are given prominence of this remarkable scholar. An important point to note is that Baghdad as the world capital had very high prices even for basic necessities which were not affordable for a poor student. Furthermore, there was no agricultural land in the city where the Shaykh could work as was the case in Jilan. These were bleak times and in the Shaykh's words: "I stayed in Baghdad for twenty years, but I could not find the means to sustain my survival."[12] After having not eaten for a few days he went outside the city to the ruins of the Persian Palace (*Iwān Kisrā*), but found a multitude of hungry people trying to eat from the measly portion of food. Malnourished and fatigued he decided against joining them believing that it was against the decorum of chivalry (*muru'ah*)[13] to do so. Therefore, he turned back to the city and went straight to a mosque after suffering bouts of total fatigue and exhaustion. After a while a man of Persian origin entered and began to eat a meal of roast meal and bread. Although extremely hungry the Shaykh exerted himself to exercise self-control. The Persian man, noticing the Shaykh, requested him to partake of the meal; however, he refused even in these straitened circumstances. The man insisted and after several requests the Shaykh finally

---

[12] *Qalā'id al-Jaw ā'hir*, 35. Cf. Al-Asqalānī, *Ghibta al-Nazir*, 12-5.
[13] *Muru'ah* refers to courage, patience and endurance, singular traits in the *tasawwuf* tradition.

accepted. In the course of their conversation the man found out that the Shaykh was the Abdul Qadir of Jilan for whom he was entrusted with the money by his pious mother. His countenance changed as he related his personal difficulties he encountered on his journey to Baghdad and using some of the money with which he bought the meal they were both eating. The Shaykh put the man at ease and even gave him a part of the money.[14]

A number of students were studying *fiqh* at Shaykh Mukharrimi's *madrasah* and it was routine that they would go to village outside Baghdad to beg for grains at the time of harvest. The Shaykh accompanied them on one occasion after much persistence by his peers. The landlords would distribute these grains as a form of *sadaqah* (charity) hoping to earn divine rewards. In the village the Shaykh met an elderly man Sharif Ya'qubi who intuitively recognised his noble personality. Addressing the Shaykh, he remarked: "Seekers of truth and pious people never beg; they don't stretch their hand before anyone. You are especially graced and favoured by the Most Gracious (*Rahmān*). It does not behove you to stretch your hand before anyone except Allah."[15]

The above incidents reveal the spirit of *istighnā* (independence) and *tawakkul* [16] (reliance on Allah) of the Shaykh. These hardships were meant to develop higher levels of *taqwā* and to face the formidable challenges of the day in his decades-long stay in Baghdad. The Shaykh recounted the solace he received from reciting the following verses (*āyāt*) in

---

[14] *Qalā'id al Jawāhir*, 35. Cf. Shattanwafi, *Bahjat al-Asrar*
[15] Cited in Qadri, *The Sultan of the Saints*, 60.
[16] *Tawakkul* in its fullest sense is a station (*maqām*) in which everything and every affair is entrusted to Allah.

his moments of extreme difficulties:

So truly with hardship comes ease
Truly with hardship comes ease. (94: 5-6)

"I would sometimes feel the weight of many burdens, heavy enough to make the mountains disintegrate, if they had been laid upon them. So, when those pressures multiplied upon me, I would set my forehead on the ground and recite the above verses.

Then I would raise my head, and to my great relief, I would always find that those heavy pressures had been chased away from me."[17]

Two salient features marked the Shaykh's spiritual journey: his spiritual retreat or seclusion (*khalwah*) and several tests of his *taqwā* which in reality attested to his growing stature as a *faqih* (jurist) tempered with *tarbiyyah* (moral training). According to several sources these were prolonged periods of seclusion.[18]

The seclusion in the wilderness outside Baghdad entailed *mujāhadah* (moral and spiritual exertion)[19] and in more ways than one was the beginning of greater things to come. Mention may be made of two incidents to appreciate the Shaykh's strict adherence to the *shari'ah* and his deep humility. Unseen help and intervention as well as divine assistance guided his response to vulnerable situations which otherwise could even mislead

---

[17] *Qalā'id al-Jawāhir*, 39.

[18] According to Hamza Malik the timeline of the Shaykh's eventful career is not consistent with the statement in *Bahjat al-Asrār* that the latter's spiritual wandering in the desert extended to twenty five years. In all probability the Shaykh did spend time in the desert on more than one occasion and the period of time could not have been so long. See *The Grey Falcon*, 84-5.

[19] *Mujāhadah* is the spiritual struggle and endeavour against passions and downward-pulling tendencies of the lower self (*nafs*). It is a ceaseless combat called *al-jihād al-akbār* (greater holy war).

spiritual guides in pursuit of moral excellence.

During one of his seclusion a cloud appeared over the Shaykh's head and burst into rain. Suddenly a luminous apparition appeared before him and proclaimed: "I am your God. I now make all unlawful things lawful to you." At this the Shaykh recited "I seek protection from Satan, the accursed." The apparition changed into a cloud and the Shaykh heard these words: "By your knowledge and by the Grace of Allah you have been saved from my deception which has led astray more than seventy seekers of truth." Satan enquired how the Shaykh had recognised him to which he replied that 'making unlawful things lawful' was a ruse. [20] The reference to the Shaykh's knowledge is a pointed one to his deep grounding in the *'ulum*, particularly *fiqh*. He was not swayed by Satan's deceptive ploys and devious plots, and more importantly, he was guided by Allah's grace (*fadl*).

The incident of the grocer illustrates the power of divine assistance. Too often incidents of this nature are dismissed as incredulous, implying a rejection of Allah's *qudrat* (power). The Shaykh recounted the following incident:

I was in the desert revising my lesson in *fiqh* in difficult circumstances when I heard a voice of a man telling me to borrow enough money while I was studying. I replied: "How am I to borrow, when I am so poor and can never repay the loan?" He answered: "Borrow and we undertake the payment." So, I went to a grocer and said to him: "Would you do business with me on the condition that I am to pay you whenever Allah eases my way, while if I die, I am absolved of payment?" The man burst into

---

[20] Salik, *The Saint of Jilan*, 19-20.

tears and said to me: "Sir, I am at your service." So, I took some provisions from him for a certain time till I could endure it no longer (regarding the burden of repayment). Then, a voice instructed me: "Go to a certain place, take whatever you find on the pile of rubble and give it to the grocer." When I went to the place as instructed, I noticed a large piece of gold on the pile of rubble, so I picked it up and gave it to the grocer[21].

In the Realms of Spirituality

Before we discuss the formative influence of *tasawwuf* on the Shaykh, two predecessors may be mentioned to illustrate the impact of the *shari'ah-tariqah* synthesis in Baghdad.

Ma'ruf al-Karkhi (d. 815) is a central figure in the development of *tasawwuf,* particularly in Baghdad. He is credited for deepening the mystical experience within the *shari'ah* ambit. The following incident highlights the moral lessons he instilled to an offender. A woman stole his prayer rug and Qur'ān while he was engaged in *salāh*. After the completion of the prayer, he ran after her asking her to return these invaluable possessions. He also lowered his gaze in keeping with the dictates of the *shari'ah*. The woman was astonished that he did not reprimand her for the offence; instead, he asked her to keep the prayer rug and return the *Mushaf* (the Qur'ān).[22] There was a hidden wisdom in the Shaykh's action: the woman was likely to make repentance (*tawba*) and start reading *salāh* regularly. Additionally, it was indicative of Ma'ruf

---

[21] Cited in Manzoor Ahmad Bhat, *Sufi Thought of Shaikh Sayyid 'Abdu'l Qādir Jilāni and its Impact on the Indian Subcontinent* (New Delhi, 2010), 90-1. A similar account is given in *Ghibta al-Nazir* and *Bahjat al-Asrār*.
[22] Fariduddin Attar, *Tadhkirat al-Awliyā*, (Lahore, n.d.), 213.

al-Karkhi's large-heartedness and spirit of humility.

Ma'ruf al-Karkhi possessed deep love and compassion for the poor and orphans. On one occasion of Eid he was seen collecting dates, which he would sell to buy clothes for an orphan boy. All the children had new sets of clothes for the occasion. In this way he brought cheer to the boy so that he could play with the other children.[23]

The *mazār* (shrine)[24] is located on the western side of Baghdad in what is known today as the Cemetery of Ma'ruf al-Karkhi.

Junayd al-Baghdadi

The Imam of his times (*Imām al-Zamān*), Junayd al- Baghdadi (d.910) was an eminent *'alim* and shaykh who acquired the highest standards of *'ulum* in his days. He was fastidious about following the *shari'ah* meticulously and critiqued the sufis who were lax in this regard. One of his famous sayings about the sufi path is as follows: "Whoever does not memorise the Qur'ān and write *hadith* is not fit in this matter. For our science (*tasawwuf*) is controlled by the Book and the *Sunnah*."[25]

Junayd al-Baghdadi strongly believed that a novice (*salik*) had to receive his moral training under a spiritual guide (*murshid*) to pursue the path of *ihsān* (moral excellence).[26] To illustrate this point: One of his disciples (*murīd*) bragged that he had achieved spiritual perfection and, therefore, there was no need

---

[23] *Masālik al-Sālihin,* vol. 1, 287.

[24] The words *mazār, dargah, maqbarah* are interchangeably used in sufi literature. These words are commonly used in geographic locations and have a rich cultural history.

[25] Gibril Fouad Haddad, *Al-Junayd Al-Baghdadi,* 1.

[26] *Ihsān* involves excellence or perfection or sanctifying virtues with inner beauty. It entails worshipping with total presence of the heart so that one is actually seeing his Lord (*Rabb*), Allah.

for a mentor, in this case a saint. He commenced with his own practice of *khalwah.* He proclaimed in the town that a retinue of angels came with a decorated camel that took him to his journey to the heavens. When Junayd al-Baghdadi was apprised about the disciple's blasphemous remarks, he decided to stay with him for a night. He asked him to make the following statement to the 'angels': "Messengers of the devil, be damned!" It was not long before he saw the so-called angels and the camel disappear. Bewildered, he saw himself seated on a pile of rubble littered with skeletons and skulls of dead bodies around him. Immediately he made *tawba* and renewed his spiritual ties (*bay'ah*) with his *murshid.* Junayd al-Baghdadi's wise counsel has salience for all: "Solitude for a novice is fatal. The company of the enlightened guide is essential in this spiritual journey."[27]

Junayd al-Baghdadi is buried in the western side of Baghdad.

Abul Qasim al-Qushayri (d. 1074), a prominent *hadith* and *tafsir* scholar, echoes similar thoughts of Junayd al-Baghdadi about the purpose of seclusion. He says:

> To seclude himself properly, a man should acquire knowledge of the religious sciences (*'ulum*) to correct his conviction (*yaqin*) in God's Oneness (*tawhīd*) so that Satan does not tempt him with his whisperings. He should also acquire knowledge from the legal sciences (*fiqh*) as to what is incumbent upon him so that the building of his affairs be on a firm foundation. Seclusion in truth is separation from reprehensible qualities and its effect is designed to change those characteristics...[28]

---

[27] Attar, *Tadhkirat al-Awliyā* (Abridged from the English translation), 116-7.

[28] Abul Qāsim al-Qushayri, *Principles of Sufism.* Translated from the Arabic

Shaykh Hammād al-Dabbās

There are three significant encounters with Hammād al-Dabbās[29] relating to the Shaykh's preparatory phase into the realms of *tasawwuf.* These were not isolated incidents, but deliberate efforts by Shaykh Dabbās to induct the Shaykh into the true essence of *ihsān.*

After a tumultuous period in Baghdad, the Shaykh desired to depart from the city on numerous occasions, but his conscience held him back. He was fully aware that his stay in Baghdad had a specific purpose: to acquire knowledge and grow spiritually. Moreover, he was fully aware that he could be of invaluable help to the people in the city which was exposed to the vagaries of political turmoil with the result that a state of decay had already set in. On one occasion he reached the Halaba Gate[30] and was about to exit when someone asked him where he was going and then gave him such a push causing the Shaykh to fall down. This mysterious figure ordered him to return to the city and benefit the people who were in dire need of spiritual guidance. Later the Shaykh discovered that the unknown person was Hammād al-Dabbās.[31]

During this period of spiritual wandering the Shaykh experienced many states (*ahwāl*)[32] which often led him to fits of

---

Al-Risāla (Berkely, 1992), 20.

[29] For a biographical note on the distinguished Shaykh Hammad al-Dabbas, see Jāmī, *Nafahat al-Uns* (Lucknow, 1915), 456-8.

[30] The Halaba Gate is now known as the Talsim (Talisman) Gate.

[31] D. S. Margoliouth, *Contributions to the Biography Of 'Abd Al-Kadir of Jilan* (London, 1907), 302.

[32] These spiritual states are gifts from Allah to heart of the seeker or traveller (*sālik*). Each sate (*hāl*) contains a myriad of subtle allusions (*ishārāt*) with innumerable meanings.

ecstasy. These conditions were interpreted by outside observers as bouts of insanity. On one occasion the Shaykh screamed uncontrollably when he was overcome by a fit of ecstasy. A notorious group of criminals dubbed as Ayyārūn who roamed outside Baghdad at night were terrified by the scream and decided to investigate. They came to where the Shaykh was and immediately recognise him as Abdul Qādir al-Majnūn.[33] Many people who had a faint idea of *tasawwuf* did not understand the spiritual experience of the Shaykh and, therefore, considered him to be *majnun* (mad). For the Shaykh these states were disturbing and he wished he could meet someone who could help him remove them. During this time, the Shaykh was passing through the Zafariyyah Quarter of Baghdad when a man abruptly asked what he had been seeking the previous day. The Shaykh was confused and remained silent for a while. The man became angry and slammed the door. The Shaykh remembered about his states and tried to locate the whereabouts of the person. He could not recognise the door. Again, it was Shaykh Dabbas who afterwards would clear all his doubts and explain to him deeper meanings of spiritual matters.[34]

A final break for the Shaykh to enter the spiritual fold of Hammād Dabbās came in an apparently severe way. By the Shaykh's admission, Hammād Dabbās would treat him badly, often beating him. However, this was all part of *tarbiyyah* (moral training) and spiritual nurturing. The moulding of the Shaykh was central to his future role as the reformer of Islam. One account refers to the disciples of Hammād Dabbās mocking the Shaykh as a mere jurist who did not belong to the *halaqah* (circle)[35] of this influential guide. As soon as Hammād

---

[33] Al-Asqalānī, *Ghibta al-Nazir*, 14.
[34] Bhat, *Sufi Thought*, 92.
[35] This is a spiritual gathering in which members of a *tariqah* devote themselves to the

Dabbās saw them trying to hurt the Shaykh's feelings, he would rise to the latter's defence and say: "O you dogs, you must not hurt his feelings! By Allah, there is not a single one like him amongst you. When I try to offend him, I only do so in order to test his mettle, for I see him as a mountain that cannot be shaken."[36]

Abu Sa'id al-Mukharrami

A doyen among the scholars in Baghdad, Abu Sa'id al-Mukharrami was the leading Hanbali jurist-sufi of his time. The Shaykh attained completion in the *tasawwuf* path through this famed guide and was granted authorisation (*ijāzah*) as well. Shaykh Mukharrami's line of transmission or *sanad* is traced through Ma'ruf al-Karkhi and Junayd al-Baghdadi which is linked to Caliph 'Ali. Other distinguished sufis are mentioned in the *sanad*, illustrating the exemplary spiritual lineage of the Shaykh.[37] In the *tasawwuf* tradition the *khirqa* or patched frock serves as a symbol of spiritual perfection.[38] The Shaykh was invested with it by his guide as the epitome of his moral and spiritual excellence. It was also a manifestation of the Shaykh's pre-eminent position as the perfect guide (*al-murshid al-kāmil*) in the metropolis and beyond.

The Shaykh was nurtured by these *mashā'ikh*[39] in preparation for his future role as the embodiment of the *shari'ah-tariqah* tradition. In this rigorous journey the Shaykh had to face trials that tested the perfection of his moral and spiritual upbringing

---

remembrance (*dhikr*) of Allah.

[36] *Qalā'id al-Jawāhir*, 50.

[37] Cited in Malik, *The Grey Falcon*, 82-3.

[38] Qadri, *The Sultan of Saints*, 76.

[39] The term *mashā'ikh* (sing. *shaykh*) denotes a spiritual teacher, mentor and guide.

– a test that revealed his unwavering faith (*yaqin*) in the *shari'ah* which stood as a bedrock against the deviant and satanic forces. Commenting on the sources of the *shari'ah*, the Shaykh says:

We have no Prophet other than him, so let us follow him, and no Book apart from the Qur'ān, so let us act upon it. Beware of your desires and the devil lest it will only lead you astray. As Allah (Exalted is He) has said:

Follow not desire, lest it leads you astray from Allah's path.

(38: 26)

Safety comes with the Book and the *Sunnah*, and destruction with all, but these two.[40]

The multifaceted role of the Shaykh is examined in the next chapter.

---

[40] Shaikh 'Abd Al-Qādir Al-Jilāni, *Futuh al-Ghaib: Revelations of the Unseen*, 96.

CHAPTER THREE

Teaching and Spiritual Profile of the Shaykh: Exemplary Islamic Scholar

Before we attempt to discuss the multi-layered teaching role of the Shaykh in the *madrasah* of his mentor, Shaykh Mukharrami, it will be helpful to give an overview of his mastery over an array of the Islamic *'ulum* (subjects) which he acquired from the famous scholars of his time.

In 511H (*hijri*) the Shaykh returned to Baghdad after having spent extensive years of study and perfecting his spiritual profile (*ruhāniyat*) – two qualities which earned him immortal fame. As a site of higher Islamic learning, the *madrasah* of Shaykh Mukharrami stood as a beacon of light illuminating the city with Islamic knowledge and culture. Several biographical sources[1] state that the Shaykh had enhanced the image of this prestigious academic institution through his vast knowledge of *tafsir, hadith, fiqh* and *sirah* in addition to his exceptional grasp of Arabic literature. In deference to the presence of his mentor the Shaykh kept a low-key profile. However, his widespread fame is a telling account of the ocean of knowledge he possessed which attracted students and scholars from the Muslim world. A graphic account is given in these words:

Our master (the Shaykh) used to lecture on thirteen branches of religious knowledge (*'ilm*). In his *madrasah*,

---

[1] The *Tārikh al-Islām al-Kabir* by Muhammad Al-Dhahabi (d. 1348) is a case in point. The work devotes a substantial section to the life and thought of the Shaykh, quoting reliable sources of scholars who were contemporaries of the Shaykh.

he would give a lesson devoted to the established legal doctrine of a particular school (*madhhab*), and a lesson devoted to differences of scholarly opinion (*ikhtilāf*). He held classes at both ends of the day, on a wide range of subjects including the rules of grammar (*nahw*). In the period following the mid-day prayer (*zuhr*), he provided instruction in the recitation of the Glorious Qur'an according to the various traditional modes of recitation (*qirā'āt*).[2]

In matters of *fiqh*, the Shaykh followed the Hanbali school of jurisprudence and was also competent in Shafi'i *fiqh*.[3]

Apart from his busy academic preoccupation the Shaykh did not neglect to follow the *Sunnah* of marriage. At the age of 51 he married four wives who were compatible with his religious inclination and temperament. He had forty-nine children, of whom were twenty-seven sons and twenty-two daughters. He was so meticulous in following the *Sunnah* in its minutest detail that even the food prepared for him reflected his strict observance and extreme love for the Holy Prophet (pbuh). It is said that the grain was particularly cultivated for his purpose.[4] This large family had made their mark in disseminating the teachings of the Shaykh. Although the Qādiri order was posthumously named after him, there were visible signs of some of his prominent sons recording his sermons and reaching out to a wider audience beyond Baghdad. A brief comment of two of his sons illustrate their singular contributions to the spread

---

[2] At-Tādifi, *Qalā'id al-Jawāhir*, 179 (Adapted).
[3] Likewise, the Shaykh had a thorough grasp of Hanafi *fiqh*. See *Mukhtasar fi 'Ilm ad-Din* authored by the Shaykh.
[4] Nasr, *Islamic Spirituality: Manifestations*, vol. 2, 12.

of the Qādiriyyah order.

Shaykh 'Abdul Wahhāb (d. 593H)

Two Hanbali scholars, Ibn Rajab and Al-Dhahabi have given excellent accounts in their widely-acclaimed works on the life and thought of Shaykh 'Abdul Wahhāb who achieved great distinction in the various fields of Islamic knowledge. He was an outstanding jurist (*faqih*) and exceptionally brilliant as a *mufti*. After the Shaykh's death he continued to deliver sermons which were infused with the sweetness of expression and a gentle sense of humour. In recognition of his legal expertise, he was often consulted by the Supreme Council of State to investigate cases of wrongdoing and injustice, which he carried out with great diligence.

Shaykh 'Abdur Razzāq (d. 603H)

A remarkable figure and influential sufi, Shaykh 'Abdul Razzāq was a noted scholar in *fiqh* and *hadith* studies. After having studied under the Shaykh in *fiqh* his quest for knowledge spurred him to gain mastery over the other branches of *'ulum* from illustrious scholars of the day. Detached from worldly possessions, Shaykh 'Abdur Razzāq took extreme care of the poor and vulnerable in Baghdad – an admirable quality that stood out in the life of the Shaykh. His teaching lessons, in particular, *hadith*, earned him fame in Baghdad and beyond.[5]

Of special significance was Shaykh 'Abdur Razzāq's close spiritual affinity with his father. In several instances the major works of the Shaykh were compiled, collated and edited by him.

---

[5] *Ibid.*, 176-83.

Key themes in the Shaykh's discourses are dedicated to him and resonate with spiritual message. Another feature of these works is the *wasiyya*[6] or a testament in sufi parlance of the Shaykh which addresses his son, Shaykh 'Abdur Razzāq.

The fame of this distinguished scholar can be gauged from the throngs of mourners who accompanied his funeral. In fact, multiple *janāza* prayers were held for him before he was buried at the Battle Gate (Bab al-Harb) in Baghdad.

These two sons exemplified the significance of the *shari'ah* in the lives of the Muslim community. They drew their inspiration from their noble father who emphasised the importance of studying *fiqh* in preparation for spiritual progress. According to the Shaykh the outer (*zāhir*) and inner (*bātin*) aspects of *fiqh* are complementary and any attempt to separate them does not produce the desired result of gaining closeness to Allah. The tendency among pseudo-sufis to exaggerate the inner aspect (*fiqh al-bātin*) has been in many ways responsible for the aversion of *tasawwuf* in Islamic reformist thought.[7]

It is evident that specialised knowledge of the *shari'ah* combined with the inner aspects of *tasawwuf* highlighted the pedigree of the Shaykh's family.

The Second Phase

After the death of Shaykh Mukharrami, the *madrasah* was left in the possession of the Shaykh. Essentially, he was an illustrious scholar with exceptional legal expertise which he combined with his teaching of *tafsir, hadith,* Arabic grammar, etc. Likewise, his discourses attracted throngs of *'ulama,* scholars

---

[6] See Shaikh 'Abd Al-Qādir Al-Jilāni, *Mukhtasar fi 'Ilm ad-Din: The Summary of Religious Knowledge and Pearls of the Heart,* 161-68.
[7] *Ibid.,* 53.

and ordinary people who were overawed by his charismatic personality. In the realm of *tasawwuf* he had no peer and this was attested by scholars and sufis alike.

With the expansion of the *madrasah* in 528H/1134, the Shaykh found a permanent home for his family within the complex. In line with his vision of training *sālikin* (aspirants in the spiritual field) the *ribāt* or *khanqah* became the spiritual lodge for them. His day would consist of teaching, preaching in open lectures and spending substantial time with his disciples (*murīds*) in the *ribāt*.[8] He then spent the next thirty-two years in teaching and preaching in the *ribāt*. When he died in 1166, the Shaykh was buried in the *madrasah's* portico, which became the nucleus of the subsequent shrine.[9] The *madrasah* complex passed into the care of Shaykh 'Abdul Wahhāb who played a leading role in the dissemination of the Shaykh's teachings and formulating in a systematic manner the Qādiriyyah *silsilah*.[10]

The Shaykh's manifold activities in teaching were remarkable for their breadth and scope. He taught thirteen subjects in the *madrasah* which of course required specialised knowledge, expertise and experience. In addition, he was able to give legal rulings (*fatāwā*) in accordance with the Hanbali and Shafi'i schools of law. Even complex questions were answered by him with relative ease. His son Shaykh 'Abdul Razzāq narrated an anecdote which underscored his father's deep scholarly acumen. A *fatwā* came to Baghdad with regard to a man who had taken a religious oath (*qasam*) to divorce his wife unless he was able to perform an act of worship (*'ibādah*) which one person (only) in

---

[8] Ibn Jawzi, *Mir'at al-Zamān*, 165.

[9] Noorah Gailani, *The Shrine of 'Abd al-Qādir al-Jilāni in Baghdad* (2015), 99.

[10] The term *silsilah* is interchangeably used for a sufi order or *tariqah*. It envisions a path or an unbroken chain that connects the *mashā'ikh* to the spiritual lineage leading up to the Holy Prophet (pbuh).

the world would be engaged in its performance at that particular time. All the scholars which included distinguished *muftis* were baffled at the nature of this intricate question and could not cite an appropriate response that would fit the criteria. When the query was brought to the Shaykh, he answered that "the man must make seven circumambulations (*tawāfs*) of the *Ka'bah* in the holy sanctuary (*haram*) of Makkah, while nobody else was doing it, and that he would be freed from his oath."[11] This spontaneous answer by the Shaykh marked out his unsurpassed knowledge in legal rulings (*iftā*).

It is generally assumed that the Shaykh was a strict advocate of the Hanbali school of law and extended occasionally his legal rulings in the light of Shafi'i school of law. This biased statement does not take into account his proficiency in Hanafi *fiqh* as outlined in his important work on the five fundamentals of Islam.[12] Consider the following statement regarding the impact of faith (*imān*) by Abu Hanifa: "Three sins pose the greatest danger of robbing one's faith:

(1) failure to give thanks (*shukr*) for the blessed grace of faith,
(2) failure to perform the obligatory religious duties (*farā'id*), and
(3) wrongful treatment of the servants (of the Lord)."[13]

The Shaykh makes a profound comment in these words:

---

[11] Cited in Malik, *The Grey Falcon*, 92-3.
[12] See Al-Jilāni, *The Summary of Knowledge*, 13-51 which also makes reference to the Hanafi position concerning the five fundamentals of Islam.
[13] *Ibid.*, 7.

Faith resembles a lamp (*sirāj)*, and compliance with the commandments and prohibitions of the *shari'ah* is comparable to taking good care of the lamp, by installing it in a lighthouse. The whispering of the devil, at the time of exposure, is comparable to the blowing of violent winds. If someone kindles the lamp of faith in his heart, but does not take good care of it, by regular performance of the acts of worship *('ibādah)* and abstinence from forbidden things, there is reason to fear that his lamp may be extinguished by the winds of the satanic whisperings (*waswās shaytāniyyah).*[14]

In his noteworthy work on the *shari'ah* and *tasawwuf* synthesis, the Shaykh elaborates on the differences of opinion (*ikhtilāf*) among the Imams on *fiqh*-based issues in the light of his vast knowledge. Interestingly, he approaches a particular issue (*mas'ala*) from a spectrum of differing opinions, revealing his juristic preference that is closest to the *Sunnah*. Again he outlines the various interpretations that also became established in Iraq and Madinah.[15]

To meet the needs of the *madrasah* complex, Islamic endowments (*awqāf*) were set up by well-wishers of the Shaykh and overseen by his son 'Abdur Razzāq. At some point, the Shaykh acquired some land that was cultivated for produce to meet the daily needs of his family, students and disciples.[16] His wives played an active part to ensuring that he led a financially independent life. In a similar vein, he was able to live off money that was gifted to him or was given as a vow for the fulfilment of a

---

[14] *Ibid.*

[15] For a detailed discussion see Shaikh 'Abd Al-Qādir Al-Jilāni, *Al-Ghunya li Tālibi Tariq al-Haqq: Sufficient Provision for Seekers of the Path of Truth.*

[16] Al-Asqalānī, *Ghibta al-Nazir*, 25.

particular thing. Even so money was spent as gifts to others. According to Shaykh Suhrawardi, the Shaykh commented that "there wasn't one of them (donors and well-wishers) that did not spend on me with goodwill and the utmost desire to do so."[17] This remark indicates the widespread popularity of the Shaykh among the rich who considered it a source of blessing (*barakah*) to support the cause of the Shaykh. Through him they were able to perform acts of charity and establish endowments to meet the growing needs of the *madrasah* complex.

Keeping in mind the widespread popularity of the Shaykh in Iraq and the Muslim world, the number of his students contributed substantially to several Islamic disciplines. For example, the famous jurisconsult, Ibn Qudama was the author of the famous *fiqh* book *Al-Mughnī*, an indispensable work to understand the Hanbali school of law. A *hadith* scholar like 'Abd al-Karim al-Sam'āni (d.1166) is listed by Dhahabi as one of the renowned scholars who transmitted *hadith* from the Shaykh.[18] This accreditation illustrates the high-ranking profile of the Shaykh in *hadith* studies, an aspect that has not received much attention by his biographers over the centuries.

In the field of *tafsir* the Shaykh was extremely knowledgeable. Several reports indicate that he was able to provide as much as twenty interpretations on a single verse (*āyah*) under discussion. Even his contemporaries were astounded by his deep knowledge in the subject.[19] There was an inner light that added radiance to his explanation of the Qur'ānic verses.

---

[17] Cited in Malik, *The Grey Falcon*, 95.
[18] Margoliouth, *Contributions to the Biography of 'Abd Al-Kadir of Jilan*, 276.
[19] Malik, *The Grey Falcon*, 93.

The Shaykh as Spiritual Guide

It will be instructive to trace the Shaykh's public discourses. In the prolonged years of *khalwah* (solitude) the Shaykh had developed a detachment from worldly pursuits, preferring a life with little, if any, contact with the hustle and bustle of the city. He had expressed his desire to remain aloof from societal life preferring the wilderness in his pursuit of inner perfection. But this was not to be – divine dispensation had planned otherwise. His mentor Shaykh Mukarrami's instruction to teach in his *madrasah* opened up new pathways for the Shaykh. In other words, alongside his teaching routine the Shaykh drew an extremely large audience who attended his *majālis* in a spiritually surcharged environment.

There was another notable influence on the Shaykh's preaching role: Shaykh Yusuf al-Hamdani (d.1140). A renowned sufi and a precursor to the Naqshbandi order of Central Asia, Shaykh al-Hamdani's charismatic presence was well known. The Shaykh's meeting with him was a turning point in his future career at the *madrasah*. He told the Shaykh as an accomplished scholar "to mount the pulpit (*minbar*) and address the people."[20] This conversation prompted the Shaykh to speak to the people by way of his discourses. In the words of Abul Hasan Ali Nadwi:

His (the Shaykh's) discourses, which were delivered on the premises of the same institution, attracted such a rush of people that extensions had to be carried out in the building of the institution. It appeared as if the whole of Baghdad assembled at his congregations. At the same time, he commanded such attention and deference from the people attending the lectures that even kings would have envied it.

---

[20] Margoliouth, *Contributions to the Biography of 'Abd Al-Kadir of Jilan*, 303.

Shaykh Muwaffaq al-Din ibn Qudāma, author of *Mughni,* records that he had not seen a man more revered for his piety than the Shaykh. The rulers, together with the chief ministers, attended his lectures alongside the rank and file and used to sit in a corner without any fanfare. Scholars and jurists rubbed shoulders with students. The enthusiastic devotion of the people who attended his lectures can be well imagined by the fact that often as many as four hundred inkpots were counted being brought in to take down the notes of his discourses.[21]

The versatility of the Shaykh in Islamic knowledge was often tested by his contemporaries. Many jurists (*fuqahā*) attended his sessions (*majālis*) to test the fame he had acquired in the Muslim world. The intricacies of the questions posed by them were answered by the Shaykh through divine inspiration (*ilhām*) and more often than not these jurists were astounded by the clarity of his exposition, brilliant grasp and depth of meaning.[22] In many instances the Shaykh probed their minds and inner motives by dispelling their misgivings about his sublime stature. A student for example had developed a flair for Arabic grammar and sat in the class of the Shaykh to acquire the advanced levels of the language. His impressions are recorded in these words:

> The Shaykh turned his face to the section of the audience in which I happened to be, and he said: "O you there! We have now become your helper, your Sibawayh!"[23] Well, by Allah, I attached myself closely to

---

[21] Abul Hasan Ali Nadwi, *Saviours of Islamic Spirit*. vol. 1, 163-4.

[22] At-Tadifi, *Qalā'id al-Jawāhir*, 136-7.

[23] Sībawayh (d. 796) was a Persian scholar of Basra (Baghdad) who made brilliant contributions to Arabic linguistics. His *Al-Kitāb* sets out the principles of Arabic grammar and still remains the standard authority.

him, and derived considerable benefit from him. I acquired a firm and thorough grasp of the principles and rules of Arabic grammar, and other sciences... I learned things that I had hardly been aware of until then, and that I had never heard from any other teacher. I received more from him, in less than a year, than I had gathered in the whole of my life up to that point. I simply forgot whatever I had received from anyone other than him.[24]

A word about the Shaykh's presentation of the *shari'ah* within the ambit of *tariqah*. Quite often there is a tendency to downplay the outer and inner aspects of the *shari'ah* by projecting an exaggerated interpretation of *tasawwuf*. This mindset in relation to the teachings of the Shaykh has produced conflicting responses which sadly have impacted on the *islāhi* (reformatory) and *tajdidi* (revivalist) role of this illustrious scholar of Islam. In the subsequent chapters a detailed discussion of his salient contributions is highlighted.

The decades-long teaching and preaching of the Shaykh had a positive impact on the Muslim world. Baghdad was transformed into a city of the saints (*awliyā*) where *'ilm* (knowledge) and *tarbiyyah* (moral training) blended seamlessly. It became a citadel for the pursuit of spiritual excellence. The political power of Muslim dynasties rose and fell; however, the charismatic personality of the Shaykh survived the ravages of time and ushered in an era of glorious history for the Muslim world.

Concerning the *hajj*, there is no conclusive evidence to indicate the exact number he performed. However, from the specific incidents about the Shaykh and his interaction with some Arab

---

[24] *Ibid.,* 133.

families in the Hijaz we can safely assume that the Shaykh was mindful of this important pillar of Islam.[25]

Sickness and Demise

In early 561H/1166 the Shaykh fell very ill and his condition deteriorated rapidly. It became clear to his family that he was near death. The advice to his son 'Abdul Wahhāb was emblematic of mission: "Inculcate a deep consciousness of the sublimity and grandeur of Allah. Fear not anyone nor cherish a desire for benefit from anyone save Allah. Entrust all of your needs to Him and then have confidence in Him. Whatever you need, place it before Allah with a conviction in the prospect of its fulfilment. Keep yourself occupied with the Oneness of Allah, on which there is consensus; for when the heart is filled with awe, love and respect for Him, nothing can escape it or get out of it." To his sons he asked them to clear the room as the angels were present and they had to be shown the greatest of respect. It appeared that for several days and night he would make *salām* to some invisible beings and would say: "May the peace and blessings of Allah be upon you. May Allah pardon you and me and accept our repentance. Come, in the name of Allah, and do not go back." When one of his sons, 'Abdul 'Aziz asked about his illness, he replied, "Don't ask me anything. I am immersed in the *ma'rifat* (gnosis) of Allah."

When asked by his son 'Abdul Jabbar about the pain he was suffering the Shaykh replied that all of his body was aching except his heart which was with Allah. He recited the following *du'ā*: "I seek help from the Most Glorified and High One, He is the Living One who never dies. Glory be to the One Who is

---

[25] See Muhammad Dawud Faruqi, *Seerat-e Ghaws-e-'Azam* (Lahore, 1979), 198.

honoured with power and who subdues His servants with death. There is no God except Allah, and Muhammad is the Messenger of Allah." After reciting this *du'ā* the Shaykh kept repeating 'Allah, Allah' until his voice grew faint. With this last word on his lip the Shaykh passed away. The Shaykh was ninety years old.[26] He was buried in Bāb al-Azaj which later became known as Bab al-Shaykh.

The shrine (*mazār*) and mosque of the Shaykh evolved over the centuries and became a major site for the Qādiriyyah order around the world.[27] It is situated on the east side of the river Tigris within the walls of the old city. The neighbourhood that surrounds it was originally known as Bāb al-Azaj.

---

[26] Adapted from *Futuh al-Ghaib*, 188-90.

[27] Noorah Gailani provides a detailed account of the shrine and mosque in terms of its administration as well as the vast network that is connected to this important place of visit (*ziyārat*) and spiritual retreat. See *The Shrine of 'Abd al-Qādir al-Jilāni*.

CHAPTER FOUR

The *Tasawwuf* Tradition: The Shaykh's Contributions

No discussion of the Shaykh's writings is complete without taking into account the ebb and flow of the prevailing political power in Baghdad. In a similar vein, the development of *tasawwuf* has a context and is traceable to the predecessors of the Shaykh whose legacy had a direct influence on his line of thought. Additionally, his charismatic personality is examined in the light of the miracles attributed to him, highlighting his extraordinary spiritual prowess (*ruhāniyat*). It should be noted that these aspects are interlinked and inseparable from a closer examination of other salient features of the Shaykh's *tajdidi* efforts.

The Shaykh spent seventy-three years of his life in Baghdad. When he came to the city, the Abbasid caliph Mustazhir bi'llah Abu'l 'Abbās (r. 1094-1118) was the reigning monarch, and after him four Caliphs acceded to the throne over a period of fifty years. This was a turbulent period for the Abbasid Caliphate, because another rival power, the Seljuqs also vied for supremacy. The rise of the Seljuq dynasty, who were of Turkish origin invaded southwestern Asia in the eleventh century and became a dominant power in the Middle East. As Sunni Muslims they set their eyes on the dominions of the Abbasid Caliphate, which gradually was experiencing a chronic decline. To give an idea about the bloodletting conflict between these dynasties, the well-known historian, Ibn Kathir gives a graphic account:

The Seljuq sultan (Mas'ud) gained victory and the Abbasid Caliph (Mustarshid) was taken prisoner. The people dismantled the pulpits of the mosques and gave up attending congregational prayers (*jamā'at*), and women came out lamenting for their Caliph and other captives. The people in other parts of the country followed suit, and Sultan Sanjar had to ask his nephew to reinstate the Caliph. Mas'ud acted on his uncle's request, but the Caliph was assassinated by the Bātinite[1] emissary while on his way back to Baghdad.[2]

The Shaykh was a witness to this internal strife and bloodshed. The scale of these feuds, the cruelty and incidence of treachery and the misery inflicted on the population for their (rulers) pleasures of power deeply saddened him. Moreover, these vices had an unsettling impact on the people who in many ways were disillusioned with the state of affairs in the country. Also, their religious enthusiasm was at its lowest. Amid the doom and gloom syndrome the Shaykh gave a clarion call for moral regeneration and purification of the self (*tazkiyah al-nafs*) through his powerful discourses.

Strands of *Tasawwuf*

Strands of *tasawwuf* in the classical period of Islamic history had woven into a dynamic and vibrant pattern that served as a

---

[1] The Bātinites were of Shi 'i origin who were notorious for the assassination of military and civilian persons, including notable bureaucrats of the Abbasid caliphate. The assassination of Nizam al-Mulk known as the grand vizier is a case in point.

[2] Ibn Kathīr, *Al-Bidāya wa'l-Nihāya*, vol.12 (Beirut, 1980), 207-8. Cf. Syed Amir Ali, *A Short History of the Saracens* (New Delhi, 1981), 337.

template for a coherent understanding of this discipline. In other words, the fusion of *shari'ah* and *tariqah* had been the guiding factor for a proper understanding of *tasawwuf.* We now refer to two classical works written by these influential sufi-scholars in this field.

Khwājah Abdullah Ansari of Herat (d. 1089) was an accomplished scholar in *tafsir* and *hadith* studies. In addition, his fame rests on his seminal work *Manāzil al-Sā'irin* (Stations of the Wayfarers) which offers refreshing insights into the inner dimensions of *tasawwuf.* The thrust of this work is the layered interpretation of Qur'ānic verses supported by the *ahādith* on the key themes discussed by the sufis in the early period of Islam.[3] The continuity of sufi thought within the *shari'ah* framework is also examined. As the title suggests, Khwājah Ansari touches on the stations that a spiritual pilgrim has to cover in his quest for spiritual excellence (*ihsān*). It must be remembered that he had written a *tafsir* containing gems of deep reflection (*tadabbur*).

Awārif al-Ma'ārif by Shaykh Shihābuddin Suhrawardi (d. 1234) resonates with the importance of the *shari'ah* and *tariqah*. In his estimation, *tasawwuf* consists "in following the practice of the Holy Prophet (pbuh) and in inculcating purity of motives and attaining the highest integrity of character."[4] While discussing the subtleties of the inner meanings of Islam, Shaykh Shihābuddin cautions against those misguided sufis who maintain that when reality (*haqiqah*) manifests itself to them then the *shari'ah* is no longer binding on them. Similarly, and have been related through the process of mass transmission (*tawātur*).[5] These viewpoints do not refer to the

---

[3] See Annamerie Schimmel, *Mystical Dimensions of Islam* (Chapel Hill, 1983), 90-1.
[4] Cited in M. M. Sharif, *A History of Muslim Philosophy.* vol.1 (Karachi, 1983), 356.
[5] See Ibn Rajab al-Hanbali, *Al-Dhayl 'ala Tabaqāt al-Hanābila* (Riyadh, 2005), 2: 188-9.

recycled and incredulous miracles that almost invest a divine status to the Shaykh. On the contrary, the miracles performed by the Shaykh have a context and are life-enriching lessons for us. They remind us that the Shaykh had a family life and followed the dictates of the *shari'ah*. Most remarkably, he was not caught up in the midst of worldly concerns to lessen his *mujāhadah* (spiritual strivings) and steadfastly followed the path that reflected the Prophetic character (*al-uswah al-hasanah*).

Recent studies have shown the general indifference by Western writers in examining the life and thought of the Shaykh. Their works focus largely on pioneering figures, such as Al-Ghazāli, Rumi, Ibn 'Arabi, etc. on account of their prolific writings. Another reason is their scepticism about the miracles attributed to the Shaykh which they have labelled as legends. Keeping in mind that the Shaykh was a strict adherent of the *shari'ah* and was not disposed to giving an elaborate and sophisticated presentation of *tasawwuf,* his popularity among the Western writers has been negligible. An important point to consider about the Shaykh's miracles is his powerful personality. They represent his unshakable level of *tawhīd,* his profound *yaqin* (conviction) and the perfection of his faith.

The nature of his miracles may take unique forms, but there is a 'hidden structure' in the incidents.[6] In other words, these miracles are a testimony of the Shaykh's spiritual stature, unveiling mysteries and occurrences that do not conform to the laws of nature.

Bhat has made a perceptive comment about the role of the reformers like the Shaykh within the *tajdidi* framework:

---

[6] For a detailed discussion, see Ahmad Munjid, "A Pilgrimage Through the Mist of Legends: Reconstructing the Life and Work of 'Abd Al-Qādir Al-Jilāni" in *Afkārunā*, 2014, 17-31.

The great sufi teachers of the time came to the rescue of Islam, which was in dire need of reform and revival. These teachers chose to reform the faith within by uniting the there are people who under the spell of delusion claim that they often converse with Allah, and as a result they receive messages which they attribute to Him.[7] This mindset violates the true essence of *tawhīd*. In respect of the mission and message of the Holy Prophet (pbuh), Shaykh Shihābuddin Suhrawardi expresses succinctly the *ādāb* (etiquettes) in these words:

> In his heart, he should not think that the perfection, rank and loftiness of character is to be found in any human being. The spiritual traveller (*sālik*) should be aware that in order to reach Allah, the path is only through his (Muhammad's) guidance. A *wali* (friend of Allah) can possess the power of perfection and guiding others only through and only from the light of the Holy Prophet's power.[8]

Shaykh Shihābuddin's reverence for the Shaykh is discussed elsewhere in the study. Here we refer to his symbolic interpretation of the rose in the Qādiriyyah order based on the following incident. The Shaykh was instructed to proceed to Baghdad. When he arrived in the city, Shaykh 'Ali al-Wāhidi sent him a cup of water hinting that Baghdad was full of holy men and there was no room for him. The Shaykh put a rose into the cup, which meant that Baghdad would find a place for him. Then all present exclaimed in unison: "The Shaykh is *our* rose."[9]

---

[7] *Ibid.,* 359.
[8] Shihabuddin Suhrawardi, *Awārif al-Ma'ārif* (New Delhi, 1981), 258. (Adapted)
[9] *Ibid.,* 285.

The Shaykh elaborated on the criteria to be met by the prospective sufi which are embedded in the Prophetic character and the righteous lives of the four Caliphs. He should always be ready to pardon and forgive those who cause harm to him. He must be endowed with a sympathetic and kind disposition which will endear him to others. To be truthful at all times and charitable are distinguishing features of his noble personality.

He should be steadfast in commanding what is right and forbidding what is wrong. Generosity and constant prayers in the night (*tahajjud*) while the others are asleep stand out in his interaction with people. To be both learned and courageous are hallmarks of an assertive believer.[10]

A closer study of the above qualities brings to the fore the Shaykh's presentation of Islamic decorum. This is a starting point for the *sālik* and is a marked departure from the rigorous conditions generally set by certain *silsilahs* (orders). In his estimation, these core values are the pillars on which the edifice of *tasawwuf* is built.

Karamat: A Brief Assessment

The number of miracles attributed to the Shaykh deserves special mention. A critical review of the *karāmāt* (miracles) has yielded conflicting positions in respect of the Shaykh's charismatic personality. Several scholars have rejected the miracles around his *tajdidi* efforts, while others have uncritically accepted them by relying on authors with questionable credentials. By and large, there is a balanced appraisal largely by Hanbali scholars whose critical studies in the *hadith* literature have earned them

---

[10] At-Tāfidi, *Qalā'id al-Jawāhir*, 55-6.

lasting fame. In many ways they represent a group of scholars whose endorsement of the Shaykh's miracles (with notable exceptions) are given prominence in their celebrated works. Ibn Rajab al-Hanbali has paid a profound and glowing tribute in his biography of the Shaykh in these words: "... sultan of the shaykhs, possessor of spiritual stations and saintly miracles (*sāhib al-maqāmāt wa'l karāmāt*)." Likewise, Al-'Izz al-Din ibn 'Abd al-Salām has said that his miracles have surpassed all the saints fragmented religious thoughts. sufism was being prepared to play a larger role, social and intellectual, ... and it was ready for whatever tasks might be required of it.[11]

Ghunya li Tālibī: Essential Work of the *Shari'ah*

Paradigm

We now focus on an important work of the Shaykh entitled *Al-Ghunya li-Tālibī*[12] which essentially examines the fundamentals of Islam, virtues and vices as well as the salient aspects of *tasawwuf*. The discourses (*mawā'iz*) are marked by the Shaykh's vast knowledge of the Qur'ān and the *Sunnah*, and his mastery of *fiqh*. Alongside these disciplines is the interweaving of ethical behaviour which leads one closer to Allah. The introductory lines to *Ghunya* explain this clearly:

> I came to recognise the sincerity of my friend's wish to acquire real knowledge of modes of behaviour which are consistent with the *shari'ah*. These include obligatory duties (*farā'id*), recommended practices (*sunan*),

---

[11] Bhat, *Sufi Thought of Shaikh Sayyid 'Abdul Qādir Jilāni*, 32-3.
[12] Shaikh 'Abd Al-Qādir Al-Jilāni, *Al-Ghunya li-Tālibi Tariq al-Haqq: Sufficient Provision for Seekers of the Path of Truth.* 5 vols.

instructions in the Qur'ān and Prophetic utterances (*alfāz al-nabawiyyah*) which are discussed in the discourses (*mawā'iz*). These practices should be useful to him in following the path of Allah and in carrying out His commands and observing His prohibitions.[13]

Overall, the work focuses on the inner aspects of Islam. The various discourses bring into sharp relief the deep reflections of the Shaykh on the Qur'ānic verses in the light of the *hadith* literature, Arabic grammar, comments by prominent scholars, etc. One point stands out: "Moral conduct (*akhlāq*) is the benchmark of a believer's nearness to Allah. It must be remembered that *Ghunya* is meant to be a guide to those who wish to tread on the path of Allah and that direct knowledge of His attributes and greatness are the initial steps. Following the outward forms of the *shari'ah* is essential in order to be 'clothed in the light of *īmān* internally (*bātin*)."[14]

A key theme underlined by the Shaykh is the importance of *adab* (correct behaviour) in relation to the five pillars of Islam, social conduct, etc. This behaviour fosters a culture of respect for the *Sunnah* both in belief and practice. A detailed discussion of the five pillars appears in this multivolume work. As an accomplished *faqih,* the Shaykh provides a comprehensive guideline about *salāh.* In fact, he is meticulous about giving the various aspects regarding the observance of *salāh* that it is no exaggeration to classify these sections as part of an essential reference work. In the Shaykh's estimation, *salāh* is a reflection of a believer's strict obedience to the commands of Allah and a means to cultivate nearness to Him as explained in the *ahādith.*

---

[13] Introduction to *Ghunya li-Tālibi.* vol.2.
[14] *Ibid.,* 98.

The motivation is very clear: *adab* removes the rust cluttered around the soul (*tazkiyah al-nafs*) and opens the pathway of inner enlightenment.[15]

Consider the Shaykh's exposition of the night vigil *(qiyām al-layl)*. First, a worshipper should ensure that his sustenance is free from the stain of doubtful things (*shubuhāt*). Second, his heart should be free from worldly distractions. Third, repentance (*tawba*) should be done in abundance.[16] This attitude prepares the worshipper to engage in *salāh* in the right frame of mind. At the same time the Shaykh cautions the worshipper to guard against drowsiness and other negative factors as these impede concentration and take away the real significance of this important prayer. In the words of the Shaykh:

> In his desire for keeping the night vigil (*qiyām al-layl*), the worshipper will also find it helpful to accustom his heart to anxiety, to grief and to sorrow, as well as to constant alertness, for in this way he will enliven his heart. He should maintain a constant contemplation of the heavenly kingdom (*al-malakut*). He should take a nap or siesta during the daytime, and avoid overtiring his physical limbs and organs in dealing with the affairs of the world.[17]

In sum, the Shaykh gives a balanced presentation of the pillars of Islam in the light of the vast corpus of literature related to *fiqh*, and his deep reflection and spiritual experiences grounded in the *tasawwuf* tradition.

---

[15] *Ghunya li-Tālibi.* vol.4.
[16] *Ibid.,* 74.
[17] *Ibid.,* 75.

Refinement of character is synonymous with *adab*. For the Shaykh, there are distinctive qualities that broaden the horizon of *ihsān* (moral excellence) which enable a believer to make significant progress in his quest for earning the pleasure of Allah (*ridd*). It is a hierarchy of values and virtues that must be internalised in the believer's life so that he may receive the *ma'rifah* (direct knowledge) of Allah. Of course, it entails faithful observance of the requirements of the *shari'ah* infused with the inner aspects of Islam termed *al-fiqh al-bātini*. This synthesis has the potential to transform a believer's life according to the *Sunnah* and be enriched morally and spiritually. The following section is a synopsis of the Shaykh's discussion on this theme.

Inner Dimensions of the *Shari'ah* in *Ghunya li Tālibi*

Let us examine the Shaykh's elucidation of *bismillah* (in the name of Allah). A cursory study brings out the structure and depth of meaning, brilliance of thought and sublimity of expression in this phrase. According to the Shaykh it possesses precious blessings: it is the consolation of our spiritual hearts, the light illuminates our breasts and gives order to our affairs. It is the name of Allah which honours certain servants and humiliates certain servants. This name inspires our minds to cultivate better and productive thoughts. Moreover, it is the name of Allah which brings solace to a distressed soul.

Based on the Shaykh's intuitive insight and levels of *ruhāniyat,* he offers refreshing insights into the recitation of the whole phrase *Bismi'llāhi ar-Rahmāni ar-Rahim* (In the name of Allah, the All-Compassionate, the All Merciful). It removes misfortunes and accounts for the special privileges enjoyed by the *ummah*. All in all, it is an invocation of Divine

Beauty within an expression of beauty.[18]

For the Shaykh, a believer is expected to do much introspection of his actions and offer repentance at all times to commit to a life of righteousness. The Qur'ānic verse is illustrative: "And repent unto Allah altogether, O believers, for then you may be able to succeed." (24: 31). It also refers to a return from all blameworthy actions to that which is praiseworthy according to the *shari'ah*.[19] Likewise, *tawba a!-nasuh* is a kind of repentance that is purely for Allah and devoid of any ulterior motive whatsoever. It means that a believer will guide his steps and always be mindful of Allah's presence and persevere through good deeds to earn Allah's pleasure.[20] There are several Qur'ānic verses that mention the virtues of repentance and for which there is "glad tidings for the believers."[21] The Shaykh urges the believers that repentance is the root and branch of every goodness, which is why righteous persons (*muttaqin*) do not abandon it. By the same token, he warns the disobedient people that they will suffer a huge loss in the Afterlife.[22] A comparison is given in these words: "Your likeness is as the likeness of a man who sells and buys without keeping account of his expenditure or counting the cash. He will soon find that his capital has disappeared and what is left with him is bad fake coins."[23] For the disobedient this world is counterfeit whereas for the righteous the world is a gem.

A salient feature of *Ghunya* is the Shaykh's systematic

---

[18] *Ghunya li-Tālibi*, 97-8.

[19] *Ibid.*, 105.

[20] *Ibid*, 10-7.

[21] For example, 9:112.

[22] Muhammad al-Casnazani al-Husseini, *Jalā' al-Khātir: Discourses by Shaikh 'Abd al-Qādir al-Jilāni* (New Delhi, 1998),13.

[23] *Ibid.*, 16.

presentation of qualities that are associated with *taqwā*. Sin is contrasted with virtue and *taqwā* with self-gratification. According to the Shaykh, the pious predecessors (*salaf*) brought out the pitfalls of pride, arrogance and self-importance in order to develop the true spirit of *taqwā*. Shaykh Junaid al-Baghdadi said that it is the excellence of character that defines a believer's spiritual stature. Keeping in mind that true devotion is following in the footsteps of the Holy Prophet (pbuh), the Shaykh makes an insightful comment:

> You must always be wary with your heart to guard against negligent lapses; with your breathing, to guard against lustful inclinations; with your throat, to guard against pleasurable temptations; and with all the limbs and organs of your physical body, to guard against bad influences of every kind - for only then will you have any hope of attaining to the Lord of the heavens and the earth.[24]

In other words, there must be a conscious effort to bring in line our physical self against the promptings of our base desires. In this regard, the Shaykh cites the opinions of several sufis to give a broader definition of *taqwā*.[25] These opinions are succinctly expressed in this Qur'ānic verse: "O you who believe, observe your duty to Allah, with the devotion that is truly due to him." (3:102). The 'rules and conditions' of *taqwā* are further explained:

> It is not piety, that you turn your faces to the East or

---

[24] *Ghunya li Tālibi*. vol.2, 213.
[25] *Ibid.*, 214-220.

West. True piety (is the piety of) one who believes in Allah and the Last Day and the angels and the Book and the Prophets; and the one who gives his wealth, for love of Him, to relatives and to orphans and the needy and the wayfarer and those who beg, and to set slaves free; and who duly performs the ritual prayer and pays the alms-due. (It is the piety of those) who fulfil their covenant when they have committed themselves to a covenant, and who are patient in tribulation and adversity and in time of stress. Such are they who are sincere. Such are the truly devout. (2:177).[26]

The Shaykh in his personal life was the embodiment of *taqwā* as mentioned in the above verse. In his spiritual wandering and prolonged years of retreat (*khalwah*) he had to face many burdens and extreme pressures which "were heavy enough to make the mountains disintegrate, if they had been laid upon them."[27] He had to bear these hardships with fortitude which on many occasions took a toll on him. Apart from the physical burdens he had to face, the spiritual crisis was more daunting. In these bleak circumstances he drew his nourishment and comfort from the knowledge that these were a trial and tribulation by Allah which would soon pass over. His conviction (*yaqin*) strengthened his resolve to continue with his spiritual exertion (*mujāhadah*) and come closer to Allah. In line with the Qur'ānic phrase - 'relief after every hardship'- the Shaykh experienced this blessing that prepared him for greater things to come. As much as the Shaykh desired to lead a reclusive life, the demand of service to humanity was an overpowering impulse. He once

---

[26] *Ibid.*, 246.
[27] *Qalā'id al-Jawāhir*, 39.

said: "I made a thorough scrutiny of all human actions, and I did not find any deed more meritorious than the providing of food, anything more noble than good moral character (*husn al-khuluq*)." [28]

The Shaykh's hospitality and generosity were proverbial. It was his daily routine to eat with guests and sit in the company of the poor, destitute and physically challenged people. He was very patient with seekers of knowledge and treated them with generosity. If any friends were absent for meals he would enquire about their situation; if anyone made him a solemn assurance or an oath, he would take him at his word without disclosing what he knew about him. His attendant, Muzaffar, would stand at the door of his house, holding the bread on a tray in his hand, and calling out: "Who would like some bread? Who would like to eat supper? Who would like a place of shelter for the night?"[29]

Ibn Najjār reports that the Shaykh used to often say: "If I were given treasures of the whole world, I would spend it all on feeding the poor." In a similar manner he would say: "It seems that I have a hole in my hands. I cannot keep anything with me. If I had a thousand dinars, I would spend every single penny by daybreak."[30]

To return to the *murīd-shaykh* relationship: The Shaykh had set out clear guidelines that fall within the ambit of *ādāb al-murīdin* (etiquettes for the seekers of the spiritual path). Our focus is on the training guide for the *murīd*. According to the Shaykh, it is essential for the *murīd* to adhere to the Book of Allah and the *Sunnah*, and 'observe them both, in practice, root

---

[28] *Ibid.*, 30.
[29] *Ibid.*, 29.
[30] Cited in Nadwi, *Saviours of Islamic Spirit.* vol. 1, 165.

and branch' making them 'his wings with which to fly' to the path that leads to Allah.[31] This is a rigorous discipline that he has to follow which will require him to exercise patience, self-sacrifice and most importantly removing any traces of self-importance. Humility should be the hallmark of his interaction with people of various backgrounds.

The modes of behaviour by the *murīd* with his *shaykh* are essential for spiritual progress. The *shaykh* makes an important point in this regard: the *murīd* has to "play the part of an advocate for his *shaykh*, against his own lower self (*nafs*)."[32] If he sees that the *shaykh's* action is incompatible with the *shari'ah* he must approach the matter in a tactful matter without alienating himself from the overall positive virtues of his guide. In the same vein, he must not believe that he possesses impeccable virtues (*'isma*) as this attitude will lead to his own ruin. If the shaykh gets angry with him or expresses displeasure over certain matters (like an offence) the *murīd* must not show any signs of annoyance or arrogance; rather, he should turn to Allah in forgiveness and repentance and resolve to abstain from repeating the offence. He must humble himself before the *shaykh*, immediately apologise for the offence committed and endear himself with the *shaykh*.

The Shaykh gives an excellent analogy of the *shaykh* acting as a link and mediator for the *murīd*. His situation resembles that of someone who wishes to seek admission in the presence of a

---

[31] *Ghunya li Tālibi*. vol. 5, 22.
[32] *Ibid*, 26.

king, with whom he has personal familiarity. He has to approach one of the king's trusted courtiers who will explain to him the protocols to be followed in the presence of the king. If he breaches the protocols then he is likely to defeat the purpose of his visit and may be looked down upon with contempt. The *shaykh-murīd* relationship is based on that singular belief that the *shaykhs* are "the road to Allah, the signposts to it, and the gate by which it is entered." Likewise, there is unbroken link to the *shaykh-murīd* relationship that is found in the lives of the eminent *awliy murīd* like Hasan al-Basri, Sari al-Saqati, etc.[33] We may cite the profound thoughts of the venerable Shaykh Abul Qāsim al-Qushayri (d.1074) in his *Risāla*.[34] He brings together the pithy sayings and anecdotes of the saints to drive home a significant point: *tasawwuf* is grounded in the Prophetic character.[35] Al-Qushayri gives an example of several saints who describe bad moral character as something that "constricts the heart, because it allows no room there for anything other than its own desires, and it becomes like a small place just large enough for its owner."[36]

Another important point that the Shaykh makes is about compatibility (*munāsibat*). It is a natural inclination and affinity to be aligned with a particular *shaykh*. Even if the paths of the *murīd* and *shaykh* diverge, their spiritual states (*ahwāl*) are decreed by destiny (*qadr*) and will remain intact. What is important is the refinement of character and developing a closeness to Allah through obedience to the *shaykh* whose guidance and

---

[33] *Ibid.*, 28-32. These illustrious figures developed a systematic formulation of *tasawwuf* and are quoted extensively by the Shaykh in his writings. They are also included in the spiritual pedigree of the Shaykh.
[34] Translated as *Principles of Sufism* (Berkeley, 1990).
[35] *Ibid.*, 301-7. This section traces the development of *tasawwuf* in the light of the statements and personal experiences of the saints (*awliyā*).
[36] *Ibid.*, 247.

companionship will lead to the goal of *ihsān*. The Shaykh elaborates:

> The *shaykh* must be a place of comfort for the seekers (*murīdin*) and a storeroom and vault for their secrets. He must serve as a refuge for them, and a cave. He must be a source of encouragement, strength and assistance, and someone who keeps firmly on the path. He must not scare them away from the path, their mutual fellowship, and their commitment to Allah.[37]

According to Khaliq Ahmad Nizami, the Shaykh laid down ten principles for the *murīd* who wished to lead a life of *taqwā*:

(1) Abstain from speaking ill of an absent person. (2) Refrain from developing a suspicious attitude against anybody. (3) Abstain from gossip and whispering. (4) Abstain from looking at things prohibited. (5) Always utter the truth. (6) Always be grateful to Allah. (7) Spend money in helping people who deserve help. (8) Abstain from running after worldly power and status. (9) Offer five times prayer regularly. (10) Follow the *Sunnah* and cooperate with Muslims.[38]

The above principles are distilled from the Shaykh's brilliant exposition of *tasawwuf* in *Ghunya*.

It was not unoften that that people with an inclination to lead a reclusive life (*khalwah*) would be mesmerised in the presence of the Shaykh. The case of Al-Jubba'i is instructive. He had resolved to isolate himself from people, spend his life in a spiritual lodge (*zāwiya*) and be fully engaged in worship (*'ibādah*). Once he prayed *sa!dh* behind the Shaykh. After the

---

[37] *Ibid.*, 41.
[38] Nasr, *Islamic Spirituality: Manifestations*, 18.

prayer, he sat in front of the Shaykh, who told him: "If you propose to be in isolation (*khalwah*), do not seclude yourself until you are suitably prepared for it. You need to spend time in the company of the *shaykhs*, and receive training from them, for only then it would be appropriate for you to practise seclusion. Otherwise, if you go off and seclude yourself before you are suitably prepared for it, you will be a chicken that has not yet grown its feathers. If you encounter some difficult problem in connection with *dīn*, you must therefore come out from your place of retreat, and seek advice of people qualified to address your *dīnī* concerns."[39] For the Shaykh, people who believed in practising seclusion should be like a candle, the light which is a source of illumination. Simply put, they should be a source of guidance for others. In another work the Shaykh highlights the influential role of the spiritual guide in these words:

> The best course is to find a true spiritual teacher who will bring your heart to life. They will secure you the eternal life of the Afterlife. This is urgent; it has to be done immediately in this life before the time is spent. This world is the field of the Afterlife. He who does not plant here will not reap there. So, plant your field upon this earth with both the subjective seeds of a good life here and the objective seeds that will yield a good harvest in the Afterlife.[40]

The Shaykh was a perfect guide and was known for his charisma and intuitive insight (*kashf*). It was a spiritual unveiling through which he could perceive the hidden motives of people

---

[39] *Qalā'id al-Jawāhir*, 123-4.
[40] Jilāni, *The Secret of Secrets*, 50.

and probe their hidden thoughts. There were occasions where streaks of egoism would overcome *murīds* who would want to exhibit their spiritual state (*hāl*). A young man attempted to show off his spiritual prowess by flying into the air. He was saying within himself: "In the whole of Baghdad there is no other man like me." It was the Shaykh who stripped him of his spiritual state and brought him down lying flat on his back.[41] The Shaykh was endowed with the power of *kashf* and with a single stroke shattered the bloated ego of the young man.

Manifestations of Worship *('Ibādah)*

Among the discourse series dealing with the outward and inner aspects of the *shari'ah* is the *Kitāb Sirr al-Asrār.*[42] It is considered a supplement to *Ghunya* and focuses, albeit briefly, on the inner points of worship (*'ibādah).* According to the Shaykh, purification (*tahārah*) is of two types: the outward is prescribed by the *shari'ah* while the inner takes into account the accumulated dirt that needs to be cleansed from the soul. This includes bad character, pride, lying, slandering, envy and anger.[43] A deeper meaning of the middle prayer generally associated with *salāt al-'asr,* according to the Shaykh symbolically refers to the prayer of the heart which is meant to obtain peace and harmony. Therefore, true worship is the worship of the heart. It is a supplication of the created to the Creator; it is a meeting of the servant and the Lord. Again, the Shaykh reminds us that the heart and soul are in sync

---

[41] *Ibid.,* 131-2.

[42] Shaikh 'Abd Al-Qādir Al-Jilāni, *Kitāb Sirr al-Asrār wa Mazhar al-Anwār: The Secret of Secrets. Manifestation of Lights* (Cambridge, 1992). Interpreted by Shaykh Tosun Bayrak al-Jerrahi al-Halveti.

[43] *Ibid.,* 71.

constantly remembering Allah whether a person appears to be asleep or awake. On the contrary, "if ritual (outward) worship does not unite with the inner (*bātin*) worship of the heart, it is lacking. Its reward is only advancing in rank. It will not bring anyone closer to the reality of the divine (in other words, closer to Allah)."[44]

The Shaykh attaches a deeper level of meaning to the pillars of Islam by emphasising the inner facets of *'ibādah*. For example, fasting in the month of Ramadan is meant to earn the pleasure of Allah and its rewards are from Him. Fasting also implies that one should keep one's senses and thoughts free from evil, and one's hands and tongue from hurting others.[45] In a similar manner, the Shaykh gives the inner dimensions of *'ibādah*. For the Shaykh, the spiritual energy must spread in the believer's life to give a sense of orientation, a sense of connection with the divine presence of Allah. It is through spiritual strivings (*mujāhaddt*) under an accomplished guide that he reaches this goal. In sum, the Shaykh gives a powerful message:

> The traveller is on the path, because there is a place to which he wishes to go. His attention is fixed principally upon that goal, yet he cannot ignore the importance for the preparation of this voyage. When he prepares, he must take heed not to be fooled by the attraction of appearances, and he must not load himself with luggage nor take the stops and stations as his final goal.[46]

---

[44] *Ibid.*, 75.
[45] *Ibid.*, 82-3.
[46] *Ibid.*, 120.

In the final analysis, a believer is expected to focus on this goal, which is the Afterlife and, therefore, must not burden himself with worldly distractions. The Shaykh is explicit on this issue and reiterates this message as the perennial source of Allah-consciousness *(taqwā)*.

Keeping in mind the Shaykh's *islāhi* vision, it is not hard to understand the extraordinary effect he had on people through his miracles. Moreover, these had a purpose and context. Apart from his sublime status the Shaykh possessed charisma and aura that transformed the lives of people. Allah had endowed him with miraculous powers which he used effectively to bring about a revolutionary change in society. The intellectual milieu of his times saw scholars of different temperaments engaged in *'ilm al-kalām* (theology)- a subject that had the potential to misguide ordinary people. At times even scholars who showed a flair for this subject took an extremely rational approach to matters related to *aqā'id*. This mindset had its own perils and it took a scholar like the Shaykh to reassert the primacy of the Qur'ān and the *Sunnah* in its pristine form. We may cite the incident of Shihābuddin 'Umar Suhrawardi,[47] a scholar of great repute, who experienced a remarkable change in the company of the Shaykh. He had a strong inclination towards theology and intended to ask the Shaykh first. He had hardly uttered a word in the company of the Shaykh when he said: "'Umar, this is no preparation for the grave."[48] Another account refers to Suhrawardi forgetting knowledge of *'ilm al-kalām* in its entirety and, instead, being blessed with the inner beauty of

---

[47] A remarkable figure in the *tasawwuf* tradition, Suhrawardi (d.1234) was the author of *Awārif al-Ma'ārif*, an essential book that deals with the fusion between the *shari'ah* and *tariqah*. He is considered to be the founder of the Suhrawardi order.

[48] Malik, *The Grey Falcon*, 99.

Islam. In his evaluation of the Shaykh's miracles, Dhahabi who is arguably one of the distinguished scholars of the sciences of *hadith ('ulum al-hadith)* has verified the accuracy of the Shaykh's established miracles. Another aspect of the Shaykh's miracles is its contextual relevance. In many instances, these miracles had life-turning moments for individuals and society in general and were a testimony to his extraordinary spiritual stature.

CHAPTER FIVE

In the Heart of the *Majālis*

The chapter sets out to examine the distinguishing features of the Shaykh's *majālis* and the themes contained in his pioneering works. In addition, the *islāhi* contents of his discourses which are interchangeably used for his discourses are also analysed.

Spiritual Ambience of the Shaykh's *Majālis*

It is worthwhile to reconstruct the *madrasah-zāwiyah*[1] of the Shaykh as a timeline concerning his *tajdidi* efforts. Reform and revival in a circumstantial setting gives the reader a holistic picture of the Shaykh's far-reaching impact on the populace of Baghdad. In other words, what were the circumstances that contributed to his extensive success as a teacher, reformer and spiritual guide? His multifaceted personality may be seen through the prism of his presentation of *'aqā'id*, adherence to the *shari'ah* and the broad-based interpretation of *tasawwuf*. These are interlinked and articulate organically his vision of *taqwā* at the highest level. By the same token, at the heart of the matter is the Shaykh's deep-seated concern for the *ummah* to take the lead in bringing humanity closer to the Islamic ideals that will set them free from the shackles of blind faith, materialism and spiritual inertia.

After the demise of Shaykh Mukharrami, the Shaykh was responsible for expanding the scope and function of the

---

[1] *Zāwiyah* is synonymous with *ribāt* and is also used in other *tariqahs*.

institution. Apart from his busy schedule of teaching thirteen different subjects, the Shaykh would conduct his *majlis* (session or assembly) three times a week: Friday and Tuesday evenings in the *madrasah* and on Sunday morning in the *ribāt* (or *zāwiyah*). It appears that on account of the throngs of listeners he moved to the Halaba Gate which was the third of four gates in the eastern walls of the city. The Shaykh's discourses were so captivating that people used to come to these gatherings with candles and torches on the backs of horses, mules and donkeys.[2] The lectern (podium) was transported to a place outside the city to accommodate the growing numbers of listeners. According to reliable sources "the number of those present at the session was usually in the region of seventy thousand."[3] Another evidence of his *karāmat* was that his voice was clearly audible in his *majālis* with such huge numbers attending.

To get an idea about the spiritual aura of his discourses, the Shaykh mentions that he received orders and prohibitions on what was to be said, in his sleep and wakeful moments, causing him to be restless to deliver what was embedded in his heart.[4] This condition is suggestive of the divine inspiration that he received, a guidance that is very much evident in his discourses. At the beginning of every *majlis* the Shaykh used to say: "Praise be to Allah, Lord of The Worlds" followed by particular reference to the Attributes of Allah and blessings upon the Holy Prophet (SAAS) and his family. Then he would invoke Allah's blessings for the forgiveness of sins, covering the *ummah's* faults in general. The *du'ā* was expressive of his total humility and *tawakkul* (reliance on Allah). In keeping with the Prophetic

---

[2] Cited in Malik, *The Grey Falcon*, 94.
[3] At-Tadifi, *Qalā'id al-Jawāhir*, 51.
[4] Margoliouth, *Contributions to the Biography*, 303.

prayer, the Shaykh used to recite: "O Allah, inspire us (*alhimnā*) with our right guidance, and grant us refuge from the evil of ourselves." In a similar vein, he would read specific Qur'ānic verses that revealed his constant prayer for Allah's guidance, forgiveness and assistance. The following description of his discourses is illustrative of his remarkable personality:

> Then he (the Shaykh) would start speaking of whatever revelations of the unseen Allah might cause his tongue to utter without notes or prepared text. In a few sessions, he would have memorised a saying (*khabar*) attributed to the Messenger of Allah (pbuh), or of the many wise statements that were read to him from the words of the sages (*hukamā*), so that he would begin by mentioning this to invoke its blessing, and start by basing his talk on it.[5]

The discourses of the Shaykh possessed a powerful eloquence, fiery rhetorical powers and the effectiveness of language that held the listeners spellbound. His son, 'Abdul Wahhab relates that his father once gave him permission to address the *majlis*. However, he could not stir the crowd who insisted that the Shaykh address them; the spontaneity of his words and simplicity of style had a mesmerising effect on them. It was a trivial story told to the crowd: the Shaykh related that the previous day his wife had boiled an egg for him and put it in a plate, when a cat came and playing around it, broke it.[6] Superficially, it was a simple story that had no bearing on the niceties of language that the Shaykh used to discuss about

---

[5] Shaikh 'Abd Al-Qādir Al-Jilāni, *Al-Fath ar-Rabbāni: The Sublime Revelation* (Kuala Lumpur, 1996), 188.
[6] Al-Asqalānī, *Ghibta al-Nazir*, 17.

matters of the heart. Yet its appeal was compelling due to the Shaykh's spiritual aura.

The fame of the Shaykh's discourses spread rapidly in Baghdad and beyond that on one occasion it attracted the attention of a hundred accomplished jurists (*fuqaha*) who attended one of his *majālis*. They decided that each of them should pose a single question that covered the branches of knowledge. After they were seated, they were suddenly overcome by an uncanny feeling that disoriented them. It was only after the Shaykh hugged them that they regained their composure. In his reassuring style the Shaykh answered their questions which they had planned to pose to him. It was an extraordinary feat that left these jurists speechless.[7]

The impact of the Shaykh's sermons was pervasive: scholars from various backgrounds and ordinary people swelled in numbers to attend his awe-inspiring talks. According to his son 'Abdul Wahhab, these sessions were maintained for a period of forty years, starting in the year 521 H and ending in the year 561 H. This period included his teaching schedule in the various Islamic subjects. The Qur'ānic recitation resonated in these sessions as the Shaykh was very particular about the listeners connecting to the teachings and message of the sacred text. The enthusiastic devotion of the people who attended the Shaykh's sermons can be well imagined by the fact that four hundred inkwells were used to take down notes - an exercise that helped in retaining verbatim his discourses.[8] According to 'Abdul Latif ibn Ahmad, the restlessness of the Shaykh's listeners prompted him to look up to the sky and recite lines of impassioned poetry asking Allah to grant him the opportunity of sharing the cup of

---

[7] At-Tāfidi, *Qalāid al-Jawāhir*, 136-7.
[8] *Ibid.*, 74-5.

(spiritual) love with his listeners.[9]

There are several accounts that indicate the spirit of devotion to the Shaykh by scholars and ordinary people alike. Any *khidmah* (service) – menial work in particular – was considered a source of great blessing. Eminent scholars of the day like Shaykh Baqā and Shaykh al-Qailawi would sweep the floor and sprinkle water to dampen the dust of the Shaykh's complex. They would not enter the Shaykh's presence without first receiving permission. In deference to the Shaykh's protocols of *adab* they would only sit down as a mark of respect. There were others who would pick up the saddle cover of his horse, hold it in front of him and walk a few steps with it. The Shaykh was averse to formalities and forbade them to do that. However, they would say: "With the like of this (royal treatment) he will draw near to Allah."[10]

The range of the Shaykh's sweeping reforms was remarkable. The depth of his sermons was life-turning moments for criminals who repented for their past misdeeds and by the Shaykh's guidance they turned into great *awliyā*. It is reported that more than five thousand Jews and Christians accepted Islam at the Shaykh's hands. In some instances, Christians who listened to his discourses would readily accept Islam. The story of the thirteen men from the Christian community makes absorbing reading. The Christians said: "We are from the community of Arab Christians. We wished to embrace Islam, but we hesitated for some time, wondering whom we should approach in order to declare ourselves Muslims in his hands. Then a mysterious voice (*hātif*) called out to us. We could hear the speaker's words, but we could not see his physical form. He was telling us: 'O

---

[9] Mulla 'Ali Qāri, *Nuzhat al-Khawātir al-Fātir*. Urdu translation by Iqbal Ahmad Faruqi (Lahore, 2003),100.
[10] *Ibid.*, 79.

riders in the caravan bound for salvation! You must go to Baghdad, and embrace Islam at the hand of Shaykh 'Abdul Qadir, for the faith (*imān*) that will be lodged in your hearts, in his presence and through his blessed grace (*fayd*), will be unlike any that could be lodged in them, in the presence of any other person, at this historical time.'"[11]

We now focus on the discourse genre of the Shaykh. In the English translation the terms 'discourse' and 'sermon' have been invariably used and in many instances these have conveyed a nuanced meaning in these pioneering works. Nonetheless, these words are interchangeably used in the study for the purpose of clarity and facility. *Al-Fath ar-Rabbāni*[12] ranks as the celebrated work of the Shaykh which has been translated into major languages of the world. As the title suggests, the Shaykh "uttered his enlightening and spiritually liberating words in the Arabic language."[13] According to Muhtar Holland, translator of this awe-inspiring work, the English equivalent 'sublime' comes closely in meaning for the word *Rabbāni* in the text.[14] Comprising sixty-two discourses the work covers key themes that tell much about the Shaykh's deep reflections on matters that lead a believer to the path of reform and closeness to Allah. On a different level, the counsels are nuggets of wisdom minted by his thorough grasp of the *shari'ah* and *tariqah*. Overall, the style is direct, forceful and the lessons are life-enriching.

The timeline of the Shaykh's discourses - Shawwal 545H. Rajab 546H - indicates that these lectures were delivered in more than one year. Fridays and Sundays were largely set aside for these inspirational talks at the *ribāt*. The compiler gives us

---

[11] *Ibid.*, 76.
[12] Shaikh 'Abd Al-Qādir Al-Jilāni, *Al-Fath ar-Rabbāni: The Sublime Revelation.*
[13] *Ibid.*, xix.
[14] *Ibid.*, xiv.

the gist of the Shaykh's discourses as follows:

It was in the ribāt, in the early morning of Friday, the last day of Rajab 546H, that the Shaykh (may Allah be well pleased with him) said:[15]

The introductory comments of the discourse generally dealt with the Attributes of Allah in relation to man's needs and dependence. The thrust of the discourse was to bring to the listeners the realisation of Allah's majesty and grandeur.

In many instances, the Shaykh would make a compelling argument regarding the lack-lustre performance of the believers concerning their obligations to Islam. There was an occasional departure from the theme of the discourse when the Shaykh was overwhelmed with divine illumination. There was complete silence in the *majlis* which counted over seventy thousand people. The Shaykh's voice was amplified and was practically audible to the multitude of listeners. This in itself was a manifestation of his *karāmat* for the purpose of moral and spiritual reform.

Counsel and exhortation were in line with the overall message of the Shaykh. Likewise, there was context for every discourse: the young man, the masses, etc. If the Shaykh spoke in affectionate terms, he was likewise stern when he addressed those that lacked knowledge, the ignorant ones, the transgressors and the hypocrites. This category of people who surrendered to their whimsical desires were reprimanded for violating the commands of Allah in their inordinate ambitions for worldly fame. By contrast, the Shaykh infused hope into people who were dejected and disillusioned in life on account

---

[15] *Ibid.,* 443.

of unfavourable circumstances. As an accomplished spiritual physician, he prescribed effective remedies for negativity, loss of faith and lethargy. Overall, the tenor of his discourses was replete with the spirit of *taqwā*, which restored confidence in the believers' reliance on the Mercy of Allah.[16]

Noteworthy Works of Spiritual Culture

Matters of the heart and soul are lucidly articulated in *Futuh a!-Ghaib*.[17] The title of this work is laden with profound meaning covering a variety of topics - seventy-eight discourses for a believer to draw closer to Allah. The discourses are focused and well-developed; the themes are generally brief in content, but the sublimity of the message is inspirational. Essentially, the Shaykh drives home the point that *zuhd* (self-discipline) is possible without compromising the *shari'ah* prescriptions. By the same token, a *murīd* (aspirant) is discouraged from engaging in rigorous spiritual strivings (*mujāhadāt*) without the guidance of a guide (*murshid*). In the estimation of the Shaykh, consistency and perseverance are tools for unveiling the secrets of the unseen "as long as the aspirant observes the limits, the commandments and prohibitions of the sacred law (*shari'ah*)."[18] The Shaykh emphasises the adherence of the Qur'ān and the *Sunnah* in order to curb unrestrained and sometimes blasphemous utterances by aspirants in a state

---

[16] For a detailed analysis of this important work, see Nasr, *Islamic Spirituality: Manifestations*. vol. 2, 18-25. Cf. Bhat, *Sufi Thought of Shaikh Sayyid 'Abdu'l Qādir Jilāni*, 160-4; " 'Abd a-Kādir Al-Jilāni" (entry) in *Encyclopaedia of Islam* (Leiden, 1986), 69-71.
[17] Shaikh 'Abd Al-Qādir al-Jilāni, *Futuh al-Ghaib: Revelations of the Unseen* (Kuala Lumpur, 1995).
[18] *Ibid.*, 102-3.

of spiritual intoxication (*sukr*).[19] Sadly, there is a tendency by overzealous sufi groups to downplay the overarching vision of *tasawwuf* as clearly outlined in the Shaykh's writings. This mindset has produced a negative reaction by sincere scholars and in some instance ambivalence to the authentic teachings of the Shaykh. In this work and in his other writings the apparent contradictions are cleared up. All in all, *Futuh al-Ghaib* signposts the path to moral and spiritual excellence (*ihsān*).

Jalā' al-Khawātir belongs to the discourse genre of the Shaykh. It has an interesting history given the fact that no definitive copy was available except one in lithographed form in Pakistan. A partial copy of this excellent work was available in the Berlin library. According to Muhtar Holland, the translation posed several challenges in the light of a single version available that had to be compared, critically analysed and verified for the purpose of conveying as accurately as possible the discourses under discussion. There are a few overlapping features in particular with *Fath ar-Rabbāni,* but these do not detract from the originality of the work. The dates assigned for these discourses are Rajab and mainly Ramadan 546H, respectively. A noteworthy feature of the English translation is that the body of the text is printed in a strong, bold font, while the footnotes are fainter and smaller in order to provide a greater degree of clarity to this work.[20]

The introductory note to *Jalā al-Khawātir* by the recorder and given a systematic form by the compiler describe the multidimensional role of the Shaykh in the history of reform and revival. It elaborates:

---

[19] See *The Secret of Secrets* which outlines in great detail the Shaykh's vision of shari'ah and *tariqah*.
[20] *Ibid.*, xi-xxiv (summarised).

The following discourses were delivered by the Shaykh, the Imam, the most learned scholar, the pious abstainer, the dutiful worshipper, the knower by direct experience (*'ārif*), the avoider of excess, the shaykh of shaykhs, the proof of Islam (*hujjat a!-Islam*), the axis of mankind (*qutb al-an'ām*), the upholder of the *Sunnah*, the suppressor of heretical innovation (*bid'āt*)... the love of those who tread the spiritual path, the pillar of the *shari'ah*, the mainstay of *haqīqah* (reality), the signpost of the *tarīqah*, the chief of the saints, the leader of the pure, the lantern of those who travel the spiritual way, the guide, the captain of those who are devoted to their duty, the lamp of the people of devotion and purity, Shaykh Muhyi ad-Din Abu Muhammad 'Abd al-Qādir, son of Abu Sālih al-Jili.[21]

The term of endearment and reverence for the Shaykh is self-evident. Elsewhere in the study, the prominent aspects of the Shaykh's *tasawwuf* temperament are discussed in detail.

A closer inspection of the discourses reveals interesting insights. The Shaykh's addresses extended to the young men, transgressors, *murīds* and common people alike. His focus is *islāh*-oriented; therefore, his audience represents the social milieu of Baghdad of his days. In this strain, virtues and vices are contrasted in his *majālis*,[22] a barometer of the Islamic consciousness prevailing among the *ummah*.

We now present key themes of the discourses that define the multifaceted personality of the Shaykh. It must be borne in mind that the spectrum of discourses is rich in diverse topics

---

[21] *Ibid.*, 5.

[22] *Ibid.*, 217-226. The thirty-ninth discourse is a case in point.

highlighting his central concern: reform of the *ummah*. Visualise the multitude of people listening to the Shaykh's discourses which pulsate with *īmānī* fervour, extraordinary spiritual energy and a focus on *taqwā* in its broadest sense. The lectern or podium is the platform to address the listeners who by now have sat in rapt attention, assimilating the minutest details of his lectures. These may be classified as sermons, talks, lectures or discourses, but there is a common thread that weaves a powerful message-the believers' success lies in moral and spiritual regeneration. What to say of the towering figure of the Shaykh who by all accounts radiates streaks of divine illumination (*nūr*)!

Tawhīd (Oneness of the Divine Being)

The forces of worldliness had become so strong during the Shaykh's time that the entire social and economic life of the community appeared to be on the brink of moral and spiritual ruin. People had developed a tendency of depending on individuals with vested interests and influential figures of the royal court for the realisation of their worldly needs. To this end, they regarded them as 'the ultimate dispensers of benefits and harm.' It was almost as if they equated divine status to them without which no worldly benefit could be accrued. The deeper people were mired in this kind of behaviour the more distant they became from Allah and His mercy. The Shaykh by his intuitive insight was cognisant of this baneful tendency and pinpointed the materialism that had sapped the community of their devotion to the positive ideals of Islam. The Shaykh makes a perceptive analysis of this malaise:

The entire creation is like a man who has been imprisoned and chained by a king with vast authority and firm command. The prisoner has been hanged from a pine tree beneath which overflows a river wide and deep. The king is seated on his throne, having arrows and bows, javelins and spears by his side. He hits the captive with whatever weapon he desires. Now would it be prudent for anyone witnessing the scene to divert his attention from the king and expect harm or favour from the captive instead of the king? Would not such a person be deemed a fool or even mad? O Allah, I seek your refuge from being misled after obtaining Your guidance, and from apostasy after having been granted faith![23]

In another discourse, the Shaykh reminds his listeners to develop the love for Allah to the exclusion of everything besides Him:

Keep your eyes fixed on Him who is looking at you. Keep yourself before One who keeps Himself before you. Listen to Him who calls you. Seek help from Him who can save you, take you out of the darkness of ignorance, cleanse you of the impurity of your soul, and redeem you from the baser self and misleading temptations, despair and timidity. Your earthly desires are like your foolish friends who keep you off the righteous path and deprive you of things pleasing and desirable. How long would you remain slaves of your desires, temptations, greed, pride - in short, this fleeting world? How long would you remain

---

23 *Futuh al-Ghaib*, "Discourse 17", 47. (Adapted)

forgetful of the Afterlife and of your Creator, the Fashioner of everything, the First and the Last, the Manifest and Hidden?[24]

The Shaykh reiterates this point further: the whole of creation is helpless and nothing can do harm or good to a person. It is Allah alone and through His will that a thing can be done through a person or somebody else. Those who are faithful and virtuous set an example for others, because their hearts are purified with the result that their inner and outer selves are one. In other words, there is no conflict in their personality development. The *shari'ah* beautifies them outwardly while *tawhīd* and the wisdom of Allah's knowledge adorn them inwardly.[25] Furthermore, the Shaykh reminds the believers that they should cleanse their hearts from the 'idols' to which they cling in the pursuit of material gain. These objects of worship include riches, pleasures and desires. Thus, the hearts should become 'a bottomless vessel' in which nothing can be kept except the possessiveness and pride (*ghayra*) of Allah. Whatever is granted thereafter to a believer is a gift or reward from Allah so that he may be of help to those who are around him and interact with him.[26]

The analogy of the empty vessel is an apt reminder to the believers that reliance on worldly possessions becomes objects of worship leading to forgetfulness of Allah (*ghaflat*). As a result of this attitude the bond of *tawakkul* weakens, the spirit of *'ibadah* diminishes and despair feeds on the restless soul. On

---

[24] *Ibid.,* "Discourse 62," 153.
[25] *Al-Fath ar-Rabbāni,* "Discourse 13," 96-7.
[26] *Futuh al-Ghaib,* "Discourse 32," 82.

a positive note, the Shaykh makes pointed reference to those who are steadfast in upholding *tawhīd* in every circumstance and in following the *shari'ah* unconditionally – they will see what gracious favours and generous blessings they will receive from Allah. The ultimate reward is "to enjoy the delights of intimate conversation (*munājāt*) with Him!"[27]

The Shaykh did not deliver his discourses in isolation nor were they exclusionary to a particular group of listeners. It was not uncommon for him to address people who had strayed from the path of truth or those who had become lethargic in the observance of the *farā'id* (duties). Far from distilling the subtleties of *tasawwuf* to the listeners, the Shaykh would make a critical appraisal of the state of affairs of the community. Here is one example:

> O young man! Treat me as your looking glass. Treat me as the mirror of your heart and your innermost being, as the mirror of your deeds. Come up close to me, then you will see things in yourself that you cannot see at a distance from me. If you have some need in your *dīn*, then use me, because I will not show any partiality when it comes to the *dīn*[28] of Allah. My manner can be quite rude when matters relating to Allah's *dīn* are at stake. I was trained by a rough hand that is averse to hypocrisy.[29]

According to the Shaykh, there is no compromise as far as the *shari'ah* is concerned. Any attempts to manipulate or distort the clear injunctions contained in the Qur'ān and the *Sunnah* are

---

[27] Shaikh 'Abd al-Qādir Al-Jilāni, *Jalā' Al-Khawātir: The Removal of Cares*, 89.
[28] *Dīn* refers to the comprehensive aspects of man's life and not religion as it is inaccurately portrayed.
[29] *Al-Fath ar-Rabbāni*, "Discourse 5," 52.

disastrous for one's *īmān*. Therefore, the heart which is aligned to Allah's remembrance (*dhikr*) is free from all kinds of inner rust. As the spiritual physician (*hakīm*) his words have a healing effect: "Be attentive to your Lord in your private moments and when you are in public situations. Set Him before your eyes so that you seem to see Him, for even if you do not see Him, He surely does see you."[30]

The Shaykh possessed *firāsat* (intuitive insight) that could probe the minds of people who interacted with him. Often, they would come without expressing their desires or had misgivings about him. Whatever the case, Allah had blessed the Shaykh with these remarkable qualities in order to offer solace to the broken hearts, to restore faith to those who had strayed from the true path and to rekindle the love for the Holy Prophet (pbuh). The Shaykh stood apart from his contemporaries on account of his lofty position that inspired awe in the hearts of people. We have it on the authority of 'Abdullah al-Jubba'i that a throng of visitors would visit the Shaykh to seek his blessings. They would kiss his hands as a mark of deep respect. Once a youth attended the *majlis* in the hope of gaining benefit from the Shaykh's presence. He had by all accounts an odious appearance: unkempt hair, clothes reeking of urine and having no semblance of ritual purity *(tahārat)*. He bowed before the Shaykh with the intention of kissing his hands. The Shaykh withdrew his hands into his sleeve and with his powerful, penetrating gaze unsettled the young man who lost control of his senses. It was after a little while that he regained his consciousness and assumed a different personality being overpowered by an indescribable spiritual transformation.[31] The magnetic appeal of the Shaykh

---

[30] *Ibid.*, 165, "Discourse 23."
[31] *Qalā'id al-Jawāhir*, 133-4. There are differing accounts to this story.

too was immersive as was evident on a number of occasions when people's lifestyle would change dramatically.

It was also not uncommon for the Shaykh to loosen the threads of his robe as he delivered his spellbinding lectures. It was an involuntary act that was suggestive of his rapturous state. When the Shaykh delivered his talk on *tawhīd* and *taqwā*, the ambience of his *majlis* was mesmerising. In the words of Yahya al-Adib: "When I attended a session, I took with me a piece of string, and each time he plucked a thread, I tied a knot in my string, which I kept hidden under my shirt. I was one of the people who stayed on till the very end of the session, and it was then that he said to me: 'Here am I, loosening knots, while you are busy tying them.'" The statement by the Shaykh has a deep significance which gives some idea about his moments of ecstasy and his *rūhānī* state.[32]

Refuge of the Broken-hearted

The Muslim society of Baghdad in the Shaykh's time could be broadly divided into two classes. The first comprised the affluent people who were deficient in faith and virtuous behaviour (*taqwā*). In contrast, were the impoverished and downtrodden class that were endowed with faith and excellent moral character. However, they were disheartened and broken-hearted due to their dismal economic circumstances, and sometimes were envious of the rich. Their despondency lowered their self-esteem, created a sense of disillusionment- in short, they felt deprived and discarded. Amid this gloom and

---

[32] *Ibid.,* 127.

doom syndrome, the Shaykh held out hope and cheer in one of his discourses. He says:

O empty-handed beggarly people! The world would appear to be at odds with you. You are barefooted, unclothed, and unfed, broken- hearted and unfortunately evicted from every place and deprived of your longings and fancies. But do not say Allah has reduced you to poverty, turned the world against you, abandoned, maligned, or persecuted you. (This mindset makes you feel) that He did not assign the portion of worldly pleasures due to you, or did not bestow fame and honour upon you. Nor is it proper to complain that Allah has granted His favours to others, made them reputed and honoured, although they belong to the same faith as you do and are the family of Adam and Eve (Hawwā) like you.

It is really so, because you are like a fertile land on which Allah is sending down the rains of endurance (*sabr*) and resignation (*tawakkul)*, of conviction and faith, of knowledge and grace. The tree of your faith is taking root and sprouting forth its branches; its shade is closing over you, pushing out new shoots and fruits, getting higher and bigger without you providing any fertiliser to it. Allah Almighty knows what you really need. He has, therefore, assigned a befitting place for you in the Afterlife. As Allah has said, nobody knows what delights have been stored for your eyes in Paradise.[33]

There is always a message of hope and solace to those who

---

[33] *Futuh al-Ghaib*, "Discourse 25," 62-3.

despair of their lot. One striking example is the use of analogy or parable by the Shaykh to raise awareness of Allah's mercy and wisdom if He subjects people to trials and tribulations. The Shaykh says:

> The believer is secure in the knowledge that Allah (Almighty and Glorious is He) will not make him experience something as a trial unless this will result in some benefit, either for this world or the Afterlife. He, therefore, accepts misfortune cheerfully, bears it with patience, and harbours no resentment against his Lord who keeps him distracted from the affliction.[34]

Trust in Allah

The discourses of the Shaykh are replete with his penetrating vision of *tawhīd* which infused him with sublime piety, producing a total resignation in Allah (*tawakkul*). In fact, *tawhīd* is interlinked with a range of topics that describe the Shaykh's wide-ranging reforms. In his unique approach, the Shaykh describes the condition of one without the conviction of faith (*yaqīn*) like someone who gathers wood by night, not knowing the harmful objects he might pick up. If the wood gathering was to be done in the day time the light of the sun will prevent him from collecting harmful things. On a positive note, *taqwā* illuminates the path of trust in Allah.

The Shaykh describes in unambiguous terms that reliance on worldly things is akin to objects of worship. If a person believes in his own strength and resources like businessmen or people

---

[34] *Al-Fath ar-Rabbāni*, "Discourse 9," 65.

in authority then the focus is turned away from Allah. Again, the Shaykh laments the apathy of people who believe in intermediaries with Allah rather than total trust in Him who alone can change their condition that is in their best interest. In sum, Allah's wisdom supersedes the finite vision of man.[35] In this respect, "Surah Al-Takāthur" conveys a strong message

for those who are too preoccupied in amassing worldly gains and forget the consequences of their acquisitiveness (greed).[36]

The level of the Shaykh's trust in Allah can be gleaned from the following incident: At a certain point in time, the Shaykh had accumulated a debt of two hundred and fifty *dīnārs* (gold coins) to certain artisans and tradesmen. Then an unfamiliar figure appeared before the Shaykh without permission, sat for quite a while in his company, then simply handed some gold, saying: "This is to clear your debt." After he left, the Shaykh instructed his attendant, al-Hattab to deliver the payment to each of his creditors. When al-Hattab asked the Shaykh about the identity of the mysterious person, he simply remarked the person was a cashier of destiny (*sayrafī al-qadr*) - an angel who appeared in disguise to settle the debt.[37]

Worldly Pleasures

The Shaykh did not preach self-denial, an alien concept which had taken root among some sufi orders. In the same vein, he did not ask people to abandon worldly possessions to pursue a life of *taqwā*. What he emphasised in his discourses was that one should use them to the extent that he needs them,

---

[35] Cited in Bhat, *Sufi Thought of Shaikh 'Abdu'l Qādir Jilāni*, 165.
[36] Surah 102: 1-8.
[37] *Qalā'id al-Jawāhir*, 119.

without allowing himself to become a slave of his desires and temptations. Essentially, he urged people not to fall into the trap of materialism. By referring to the *hadith*: "Verily, the world has been created for you, and you have been created for the Afterlife," the Shaykh explains:

> Do not try to obtain your share of worldly gifts in a way that you have to keep standing before it like a beggar. You ought to be like a sovereign (a person in authority) who keep himself seated while gifts are presented before him. This world praises those who stand and wait at the door of Allah Almighty, but it demeans those who wait upon the world. Therefore, get your share of worldly benefits without lowering yourself or compromising your dignity. This is what Allah expects of you.[38]

According to the Shaykh, it is perfectly lawful to earn a livelihood and to accumulate the 'gifts and possessions' for a commendable purpose. However, these material possessions should not dominate a person's life or create a culture of obsession. In the Shaykh's words: "You may allow it to stand at the door of your heart, but it is prohibited to allow it to get inside, for it shall not bring any honour to you."[39]

There is a fine distinction between accumulating wealth for commendable purposes and obsession for amassing wealth for undesirable purposes. The Shaykh elaborates:

> When Allah gives you wealth, and you let your preoccupation with it distract you from obedient service to

---

[38] *Al-Fath ar-Rabbāni*, "Discourse 21," 151-4. A detailed discussion on this topic appears in this discourse.
[39] *Ibid.*, "Discourse 51," 341.

Him, He makes it a barrier between you and Himself in both this world and the Afterlife. Perhaps He will dispossess you of the wealth, alter your financial circumstances and reduce you to poverty, as punishment for letting your preoccupation with the gift distract you from the Giver. But if you pay more attention to obeying Him than to material wealth, He will make you a present of it without deducting a single atom.[40]

The Shaykh employs instructive lessons to demonstrate the level of trust by the family of the Holy Prophet (pbuh). If Ja'far bin al-Sadiq[41] needed a hundred dinars, but had no more than fifty with him at the time, he would donate all to charity. Then, sure enough, five hundred dinars would come his way a few days later. "However, even if they had not come to him, he would not have doubted his Lord; he would not have raised any protest against Him, nor harboured any feeling of resentment towards Him."[42] For the *murīds* the Shaykh echoes a similar message: " When the seeker is put to test and made to suffer, he needs a qualified doctor (*ustādh*) to treat him during this ordeal, someone who will instruct him to bear it with patience and be thankful for it, who will tell him what medicine to take, who will tell him to turn away from his lower self (*nafs*) and stop giving in to its demands. If the seeker sincerely accepts the advice of his *shaykh*, Allah (Almighty and Glorious is He) will put an end to his ordeal sooner or later."[43]

In his personal life the Shaykh showed his detachment to

---

[40] *Futuh al-Ghaib*, "Discourse 12," 34.
[41] Ja'far al-Sadiq was the sixth of the twelve descendants of the Holy Prophet (pbuh) who, according to the majority of the Shi'ahs are considered the rightful Imams.
[42] *Jalā' Al-Khawātir*, "Discourse 31," 185.
[43] *Ibid.*, 135.

material wealth. If he received any gifts by his well-wishers or upright persons, he would gladly accept them. It was his practice to distribute these gifts or dinars to the deserving persons.

It is related that the Shaykh was engaged in trade while upholding the spirit of abstinence for the sake of Islam. Once while he was sitting in his *ribāt* with his *murīds,* he was informed by his manager that the flotilla which was carrying the merchandise from Basra had perished at sea. The Shaykh looked at the manager, bowed his head for a few moments and then said "Al-hamdulillah!" (All praise is due to Allah) and continued with his discourse. After a short while the manager informed the Shaykh that the information was inaccurate as the flotilla was caught up in a huge storm, but managed to reach the shore safely. Again, the Shaykh looked at the manager, bowed his head for a few moments, lifted his head and said "Al-hamdulillah!" One of his *murīds* was perplexed at the Shaykh's reaction to which he replied: "You are mistaken in thinking that I said "Al-hamdulillah" on the drowning or saving of the flotilla. I introspected and examined my inner self to see if the shocking news or the good news had the slightest effect on my emotion, and I found that there was none. And it was then that I said "Al-hamdulillah.""[44]

This incident emphasises the Shaykh's detachment from material possessions and covers a major theme in his writings: the heart is the repository of moral and spiritual excellence if nurtured with divine qualities. To get a sense of the Shaykh's balanced attitude and his positive outlook on a believer's attitude to this world and the Afterlife, the following *du'ā* was generally read after the conclusion of his discourse:

---

[44] Abdul Kader Choughley (editor), *Moral and Spiritual Transformation in Islam* (Springs, 2019), 69-71.

"Our Lord, give us good in this world and in the Afterlife, and protect us from the torment of the fire." (2: 201)

Critiques of the Caliph and Influential Figures

The Shaykh was not sparing in the admonition of the kings, nobles and officials if their policies and behaviour violated the injunctions of the *shari'ah*. For the Shaykh the *shari'ah* laid clear guidelines of enjoining what is right and forbidding what is wrong.

The times of the Shaykh in Baghdad - seventy-three years - were politically unstable. The lust for power by various kingdoms and weakening of authority of the once powerful Abbasids were heart-rending incidents for the Shaykh. Bloodshed and feuds, treachery and savagery were rife while the evil effects of these brutalities added more miseries to the lives of the masses. In these harrowing circumstances the Shaykh criticised the faults of the great ones without the slightest consideration of their power or position. The noted historian and commentator on the Qur'ān, Ibn Kathīr made these incisive comments:

He (the Shaykh) admonished all - caliphs, viziers, kings, jurists, elites and laity – to adopt the righteous path and forsake things that were forbidden. He openly and unsparingly criticised anyone to his face in his discourses. He used to denounce the authorities sternly if they appointed a tyrant to public office. He never cared for anyone if he saw the commands of Allah being overstepped.[45]

When Caliph Muqtafi li-Amri'llah appointed Abu'l Wafa Yahyā, a man notorious for his cruelty, as Chief Justice, the Shaykh admonished the Caliph in these words:

> You have appointed a man notorious as the most tyrannical to rule over the Muslims. What would your answer be tomorrow on the Day of Judgement before the Lord of the Worlds, the Most Merciful?[46]

It was the Shaykh's policy not to entertain the presence of kings and dignitaries in his *majālis* or in his private apartment. If they happened to be seated in a session, the Shaykh would come back out and slip into his private apartment. Sometimes it was unavoidable for the Shaykh to address them in the *majlis*. He would be blunt in his speech and admonish them while they would kiss his hand, and sit in his presence with an affected air of modesty and humility. The Shaykh did not stand up in honour for state authorities.[47]

The aura that the Shaykh exuded would unsettle the Caliph Al-Muqtafi. He had voiced his concern to his Chief Minister (vizier) that the Shaykh treated him with scornful disdain. Worse still, the Shaykh mentioned him by name and said to the palm tree at his guesthouse: "O palm tree, do not act unjustly, or I shall cut off your head." The Caliph deputed his Chief Minister to meet the Shaykh in private to dissuade the latter from making these improper comments of the Caliphate. He sat in the *majlis*

---

[45] Ibn Kathīr, *Al-Bidāya wa'l Nihāya*, 12; 252.
[46] *Qalā'id al-Jawāhir*, Cf. Muhammad Amjad Husayn,*Tārikh-e-Mashā'ikh-e Tasawwuf* (Rawalpindi, 2015), 133-4.
[47] *Ibid.*, 82.

hoping to find an opportunity to speak to the Shaykh in private. During the course of the discourse, the Shaykh remarked: "Yes, I shall cut of its head." The Chief Minister was dumbfounded and left the session. He related what had transpired to the Caliph. It was not long when the Chief Minister attended the *majlis* again. The Shaykh admonished him time and again until he reduced him to tears. Then the Shaykh changed his tone and treated him with gentle kindness.[48] The Shaykh believed that *islāh al-nafs* or bringing the ego under control was essential for nurturing a good character.

The relationship between the Caliph and the Shaykh was based on counsel and admonition, when necessary. The Shaykh did not follow state protocols and boldly stated what he considered to be in the interest of the state. When he engaged in correspondence with the Caliph, he would dispense with the royal formalities (which he regarded a hindrance) and write to him: " 'Abd al-Qadir commands you to do so such-and-such. And you are aware that his command is obligatory upon you to carry out. He (the Shaykh) is your guide, and a competent authority over you.' Then having read his sheet of paper, the Caliph would kiss it saying: 'The Shaykh has spoken the truth.'"[49]

The Shaykh vigorously condemned the worldliness of those scholars, jurists and saints who were prepared to hold positions from a ruler, thus compromising their sense of independence. Moreover, he blamed this class for condoning the waywardness of the rulers and other state officials. In one of his discourses, he rebuked them for their laxity in religious matters:

You are the one who have misused your knowledge and

---

[48] *Ibid.*, 83.
[49] *Ibid.*, 82 (Adapted).

wisdom. What have you to do with your predecessors (*al-salaf al-sālih*)? You are the enemies of Allah and His Messenger; you are no more than robbers, tyrants and hypocrites! How long will you persist in your pious fraud? How long will you continue to wear this shroud of affected piety for the sake of your kings and rulers? How long will you remain a slave of power and position, passion and desires?... Are you not afraid that your greed has forced you to serve these tyrants and acquire the unlawful? The kingdom of the rulers to whom you are playing second fiddle shall be no more, and then you shall be presented before Allah Almighty, who is Eternal, Almighty.[50]

On a broader level, the Shaykh warns the believers of injustice (*zulm*) which would be enveloped in darkness and gloom on the Day of Resurrection. At the same time, he speaks about the consequences of injustice in relation to Allah's power of justice. The supplication of the oppressed person is readily accepted by Allah; the dark deeds of the oppressor are exposed and he is subjected to misery, humiliation and painful suffering in this world.[51] In the same vein, the Shaykh rebuked an Imam of the Abbasid dynasty who served as a state functionary. In the guise of seeking advice from the Shaykh, he presented a huge sum of money, contained in ten vessels, carried by ten of his personal servants. The Imam insisted that the Shaykh accept the money and pressed with this matter with great urgency. The Shaykh grasped one vessel in his right hand, the other in his left and squeezed them tightly till they began to drip in blood. The Shaykh remarked: "O Abu'l Muzaffar, do you not feel any

---

[50] *Al Fath ar-Rabbāni*, "Discourse 52," 349.
[51] *Jalā' Al-Khawātir*, 111.

shame before Allah, that you should take the wealth from the people and offer it to me?" The Imam fainted when he saw the reality of his huge sum of money.[52]

The Shaykh warns people to be wary of scholars who do not practise what they preach:

> Do not be deceived by these scholars (misguided ones) who are ignorant of Allah. All their knowledge works against them and not for them. They are knowledgeable in the laws of Allah (*shari'ah*), but ignorant of Allah himself. They command people with which they do not do, and forbid people from the things which they do not abstain from. They call people to the Truth (*al-haqq*), while they themselves flee from Him. They rebel and sin against Him with impudence. I have their names written, recorded and listed.[53]

The deviant scholars are critically analysed in the Shaykh's writings. They have a toxic influence on the masses and, therefore, need to be exposed. By the same token, the Shaykh exhorts the believers to place their trust on the authoritative *shaykhs* who are the embodiment of the *shari'ah-tariqah* temperament.[54] This is particularly true about those who have a superficial link to *din* without realising that their wealth and comfort zones are temporary things. In reality, the successful people are those who always think well of the *shaykhs*, and respect their knowledge *('ilm)* and are prepared to learn in the company of these blessed souls. For a *murīd*, he has to develop a correct attitude toward companionship (*suhba*) with the *shaykh*. This

---

[52] *Qalā'id al-Jawāhir*, 124-5.
[53] Cited in Malik, *The Grey Falcon*, 211.
[54] *Al-Fath ar-Rabbāni*, 63.

relationship will "feed him through the mouth of his heart, nourishing him with the food and drink of the kind of knowledge that is only acquired by direct experience (*ma'rifah*)."[55]

The Shaykh reminds people aspiring to pursue the spiritual path to discard their self-centred interest if they wish to benefit from his companionship (*suhba*). They should come as spiritually bankrupt (*muflis*) in order to be enriched by the gems of his knowledge and wisdom. As such there is a potential growth for a sincere person (*mukhlis*) to gain the highest level of divine realisation (*ma'rifah*) by following the *Sunnah* unconditionally. The Shaykh personified the Prophetic ideal in all aspects of his life. "If you love me, the benefit of all of this will accrue to you, but if you hate me, the effect it has on you will be detrimental."[56] This statement by the Shaykh underscores his primary role in projecting the *Sunnah* as the touchstone of success in this world and in the Afterlife. Likewise, it fits perfectly in line with his vision of reforming the *ummah*.

---

[55] *Jalā' al-Khawātir*, 97.
[56] *Ibid.*, 18.

CHAPTER SIX

Moral Regeneration of Humanity:
An Islamic Perspective

The discourses covered by the Shaykh in his principal works offer an array of topics affecting the Muslim community. We need to keep in mind the socio-political conditions prevailing in Baghdad to examine the tenor of his discourses and its impact on the world of Islam. The focus of the chapter is based on the key themes derived from his writings as well as the Shaykh's spiritual stature in the light of his pronouncements.

Man in Disguise

As a spiritual physician, the Shaykh analyses the factors that have hindered the religious consciousness (*shu'ur*) of the Muslim community. Of particular significance is the deepening hypocrisy (*nifāq*) that has taken root in society. In several discourses the Shaykh makes a critical appraisal of the mindset of scholars, pseudo-religious figures and the youth who have delinked themselves from the true spirit of the Islamic teachings. Moreover, they have developed a bloated ego and disdain for the heirs of the Holy Prophet (pbuh) - the *awliyā'*- and if these tendencies remain unchecked the consequences will be grave, to say the least.

The Shaykh uses unambiguous terms to describe the traits of a hypocrite (*munāfiq*): laxity in observing the pillars of Islam, conceit, arrogance and a materialistic outlook. In one of his discourses the Shaykh criticises the hypocrite who fakes piety in his *salāh* to attract the attention of others. He is entrapped by the guiles of Satan who makes him believe that his sincerity of worship is impeccable. Self-importance according to the Shaykh leads one to the 'heat of a scorching fire.' Another trait of the hypocrite is that he memorises the Qur'ān, but is heedless of its teachings and has no inclination to practise them. Likewise, he memorises the *Sunnah* of the Holy Prophet (pbuh) but makes no serious effort to practise upon it.[1]

The Shaykh is unequivocal in his critique of the hypocrites who feign respect for the *awliyā*. Their deep-seated arrogance is a barrier to respect the saints' position in this world. They are entrusted with the responsibilities of protecting and preserving the *din* from deviant beliefs and to restore the authenticity of Islam in all circumstances. To the hypocrites, the Shaykh has one message: approach the *awliyā* with a sense of humility to assimilate the essence of the Islamic teachings.[2] The Shaykh relates the incident of a man who came into the presence of the notable saint, Abu Yazid al-Bistami, then kept looking to left and right, so Abu Yazid asked him: "What is the matter with you?" The man replied: "I want to find a clean spot where I can perform my *salāh*." Abu Yazid said to him: "Purify your heart and pray wherever you wish."[3] The Shaykh makes a pertinent point that that the real meaning of pretence (*riyā*) is known only by the sincere *(mukhlisun)*.

The hidden defects of the hypocrites come to the fore in their behaviour and actions. In a rhetorical question the Shaykh says: "Do you feel no shame before Him (Allah), and do you not believe that the meeting with Him must come soon?" Again, the Shaykh reiterates the same message to the hypocrites: repent, make

---

[1] *Fath ar-Rabbāni*, 68-9.
[2] *Ibid.*, 102.
[3] *Ibid.*, 190.

amends for the past misdeeds and correct the intention to receive Allah's mercy.[4]

In his personal interaction with the hypocrites or people with hidden agendas, the Shaykh warned them that he could detect pretence and hypocrisy in their hearts. He says: "You are trying to keep your condition hidden from me, but it will not be concealed. You pretend to be a seeker of the Afterlife, although you are actually a seeker of this world. The delusion in your heart is written on your forehead. Your secret is public knowledge. Therefore, repent your showy pretence (*riyā)* and hypocrisy (*nifdāq*) and do not hesitate to be guilty of (these harmful qualities)."[5] It is evident that the Shaykh's approach to sinful behaviour was two-fold: highlight the misdeed and then rectify it by counsel and admonition. This approach was in keeping with his role of a reformer (*muslih*).

Love for Humanity

Love for humanity in general and concern about the welfare of the *ummah* in particular were the distinctive qualities of the Shaykh. His sublimated soul was a reflection of the noble character (*al-uswah al-hasanah*) of the Holy Prophet (pbuh). His perceptive appraisal of the different types of people brings out clearly the temperament and disposition that characterise their affinity to Islam. For example, the Shaykh describes the type of people and their reasons for visiting the market. Coming to

the last category of people, he was perhaps describing his own

---

[4] *Ibid.,* 232.
[5] *Ibid.,* 82.

spiritual state in these words:

> And there is the fifth man, when he enters a market, he is sufficiently filled with awe and reverence of the Almighty to seek His blessings for those at the market. He becomes oblivious of everything else except his compassion for the people. He remains immersed, from his time of entry into the market till he comes out of it, praying solemnly for divine blessings and in repenting for the sins of those who happen to be there, and thus, he hardly gets any time to see what they are buying or selling. His heart bleeds and his eyes shed tears over the ingratitude of man, while his tongue remains busy in thanking Allah over what He has bestowed to his servants.[6]

In the context of the twenty-first century these inspiring words are thoughtful lessons for a consumerist society caught up in the web of material possessions.

A brief comment on the *Fifteen Letters* written by the Shaykh makes interesting reading. It is actually a Persian work of the Shaykh replete with Qur'ānic verses (*āyāt*). The translator, Muhtar Holland, has given a brief overview about the Arabic version of this slim volume and echoes the sentiments of the Arabic translator, Husam al-din Muttaqi (d.1569) that the charm and expressive style of the Shaykh's writing is simply admirable.[7] The book contains approximately two hundred and seventy-five verses clustered under various topics. Muttaqi makes an important comment on the *Fifteen Letters* in these words:

---

[6] *Futuh al-Ghaib*, "Discourse 72," 172.
[7] Shaykh 'Abd al-Qādir Al-Jilāni, *Khamsata 'Ashara Maktubān: Fifteen Letters* 111, xi-xii.

Originally written in the Persian language, these letters comprise nuggets of wisdom and spiritual counsel, couched in various forms of allegory, metaphor, paraphrase and quotation, including approximately two hundred and seventy-five Qur'ānic verses. They also contain allusions (indirect references) to the experiences (*adhwāq*) and spiritual states (*hālāt*) of the sufis.[8]

We now look at excerpts from these letters to get a clearer idea of the Shaykh's presentation of the Qur'ānic themes.

In the "Fifth Letter" the Shaykh contextualises particular verses to highlight the presence of Allah. The use of metaphorical language is intended to emphasise the Attributes of Allah. The seeker experiences the rapture of divine love (*al-'ishq*), 'wandering in the deserts of his quest.' Then the yearning overwhelms him when the herald of:

Allah is truly Bountiful toward mankind. (10: 60)
-will proclaim:

And He is with you wherever you may be. (57: 4)

Once the seeker has discovered the secret of 'togetherness' (*al-ma'iyya*), he will lose his personal existence, in compliance with the dictate of:

And do not set together with Allah another god.
(51: 51)[9]

---

[8] *Ibid.*, 5.
[9] *Ibid.*, 18-9.

The "Ninth Letter" has an incentive to seek the companionship of the righteous and to practise self-abstinence (*zuhd*) from this world.

You must keep a safe distance from the perilous roads of the temptations:

Your wealth and your children are merely a temptation.

(64: 15)

You must head for the routes that follow the course of the guidance of:

This is surely a Reminder; so, whoever is willing, let him choose a way to his Lord. (73: 19)[10]

In the "Thirteenth Letter" the Shaykh gives a spiritual dimension to the verse: *Allah is the light of the heavens and the earth.* (24: 35). The 'niche of the conscience' and the 'glass of the heart' carry profound meanings pertaining to the light (*nur*) in these glorious verses.[11]

In our discussion of the Shaykh's contribution to the tafsir tradition (Chapter 7) the *tasawwuf* element is highlighted in greater detail.

In the realms of spirituality, the Shaykh had no peers. So it was with the number of miracles (*karāmāt*) he performed. These feats of miraculous power illustrated the stature of the Shaykh who deepened the true contents of faith among the people of Baghdad. These miraculous events also had a transformative

---

[10] *Ibid.*, 29.
[11] *Ibid.*, 40-1.

potential: to witness the infinite power of Allah (*qudrat*) granted to His special servants for the purpose of reforming society. And it was not uncommon for scholars and other sections of the *ummah* to seek the Shaykh's blessings or intervention on matters of pressing importance. Essentially, it was a testament to his powerful personality and his vigorous campaign for the restoration of moral and spiritual values enshrined in the Qur'ān and the *Sunnah*.

Muzaffar al-Harbi used to sleep in the *ribāt* of the Shaykh to ensure that he would not miss his discourses. Once he climbed the roof of the *ribāt* on a scorching hot day and longed for fresh dates. He prayed to Allah: "O Lord! If only I could have five dates." The Shaykh had a trapdoor in the roof, which he opened, carrying five dates in his hand. He called out by his name: "Muzaffar, find what you have desired." The narrator mentions that the Shaykh had no idea who he was and was not even familiar with his name.[12]

Another incident is reported by Shaykh Shams al-din who regularly attended the *majālis* of the Shaykh. One night he experienced ritual impurity due to the emission of semen. It was a bitterly cold night and he decided to attend the session of the Shaykh even in this impure state. After the discourse was over, he took a bath. Thereafter, he went to the *ribāt* where the Shaykh was in the pulpit (*minbar*). The moment the Shaykh's eyes fell on him, he remarked: "O twister (*yā dābir*)! You attend our session while you are in a state of ritual impurity (*junub*), and you plead the cold as your excuse."[13]

An extraordinary incident that reveals the high level of *kashf* by the Shaykh is narrated by Shaykh 'Abdullah Muhammad al-

---

[12] Bhat, *Sufi Thought of Shaikh Sayyid 'Abdul Qādir Jilāni*, 101.
[13] *Qalā'id al-Jawāhir*, 331.

Husayni. It was in Muharram 599H when approximately three hundred visitors assembled at the Shaykh's reception hall which was located in the arcade of al-Halba. The Shaykh hurriedly emerged from his private apartment and repeatedly alerted them to come to him. In the consternation they all hurried to him until there was no one left in the arcade. A few moments later the roof of the arcade collapsed with all the visitors assembled in a place of safety. The Shaykh told them: "I was in the private apartment, when I heard a voice say: 'The roof is about to collapse, at this very instant,' so I took pity on you all."[14]

The Shaykh was always concerned about the welfare of the people of Baghdad. His charming personality typified his love for humanity. If a calamity befell them, it was the Shaykh who would offer solace and make *du'ā* for their ease. On one occasion the levels of the Tigris River had kept rising intermittently for years and the city was threatened with a devastating flood. The people were always in awe of the Shaykh and, therefore, appealed for his help and prayers in this perilous situation. The Shaykh responded by picking up his staff and headed for the river bank. He planted the staff at the water's edge and said: "Up to this point, but no higher." The water level dropped significantly, forestalling the potential fear of a flood.[15]

From the details available about the Shaykh's *majlis*, the ambience of *adab* was discernible. When the Shaykh proceeded to the lectern all the listeners stood in honour of him. When he spoke, it appeared as if silence enveloped the *majlis*; the throngs of devout listeners were focused on every word he uttered. In many instances, the Shaykh bowed his head in a reflective mood. Then he raised his head and spoke on matters of the

---

[14] *Ibid.*, 132.
[15] *Ibid.*, 108-9.

heart. It was an awe-inspiring experience. Often, he would respond to the inner thoughts, desires and sometimes misgivings of listeners. They would be dumbstruck at the spontaneity of his response as if their questions were posed at a public platform. No one left his *majlis* without a sense of positivity. Again, the discourses would send hundreds of listeners into a state of ecstasy while others would repent (*tawba*) and commit themselves to a righteous life. This indeed was a transformation of souls seeking to earn Allah's pleasure.

A notable aspect of the Shaykh's discourses was the element of faith and conviction (*yaqin*) that he instilled in his listeners. On one occasion while the Shaykh was delivering a powerful speech, a shower of rain descended from the sky. This caused some of the listeners to disperse and seek shelter. The Shaykh raised his head toward the heaven above and said: "Here I am gathering people together for Your (Allah's) sake, and You are scattering them away from me like this!" The rain stopped at once where the *majlis* was taking place although it continued unabated outside the *ribāt*.[16] This impassioned *du'ā* is a testament to the Shaykh's *karāmāt*.

The spirit of *yaqin* resonates in different eras and locations as well. An incident of the rain during a speech delivered by the Roving Ambassador of Peace, Mawlana Abdul Aleem Siddiqui Al-Qadri (d. 1954) has relevance. His secretary and *khalifa* (spiritual deputy), Dr Mawlana Fazlur Rahman Ansari (d. 1974) narrated an inspiring account of Mawlana Siddiqui's *karāmāt*:

Let me tell you about Mawlana Abdul Aleem Siddiqui. I was with him on a world tour during 1950 and we visited the

---

[16] *Ibid.*, 119-20.

capital of the Philippines, Qutabatu. A function was to be held on an open square scheduled to begin after Maghrib. After Zuhr *salāh*, dark clouds appeared and by 'Asr, conditions worsened with signs of a big storm. After 'Asr, I mentioned to my teacher about the dark clouds and the rolling thunder and the impending storm, and he replied: "My dear son, why are you worried? We have come here to deliver the message of Allah - the rain is sent by Allah, the earth belongs to Allah and the human beings are creatures of Allah, and if He wants me to deliver the message it will be done."

After Maghrib we went to the open plain, where a huge crowd was waiting. The Governor was the chairman and the Chief Justice who was a Roman Catholic was also there. His Eminence, Mawlana Siddiqui just began to deliver this talk when huge drops of rain started to fall. The huge crowd started to get up in order to flee to their homes when Mawlana Siddiqui said: "My dear friends, don't be worried, the rain is going to stop right now." And the rain stopped. Mawlana Siddiqui assured them that "[it] will not rain for as long as this function is on. However, after the function is over you will have ten minutes to get to your homes, and then a very big storm will come."

Not one drop of rain fell after the announcement and Mawlana Siddiqui delivered one of his finest lectures in an utmost carefree manner and spoke for about one and a half hour. The rumbling and thunder were there all the time. Then the chairman gave the vote of thanks. When the function was over, the people rushed to the platform in order to shake hands with Mawlana Siddiqui who again said: "My dear friends, you were running away from here earlier and don't you see what is happening in the sky? Please, for Allah's sake, you have ten minutes to get to your homes and I am going to my hotel." Exactly ten minutes later the storm came and the following morning, the water in the roads was about two metres high. Thousands of those who were Catholics, became Muslims. This happened in 1950! This is *khalifat Allah* and this is *Islam.*[17]

Another outstanding quality of the Shaykh was his candid response to questions that had hidden motives. In this case he would express his indignation at these questions which smacked of arrogance. In many instances before a word could be said the Shaykh would exclaim: "Hold your tongue! I see that your question arises from your natural impulse and your *nafs.* Do not play with me. I am the executioner. I am lethal." On one occasion some persons in the *majlis* rose to ask a question which was ignored by the Shaykh. In strong words the Shaykh rebuked them by stating that they should stop fantasising as their pride and arrogance would be their ruin. In the Shaykh's words: "I only speak the truth and treat you impartially for the religion of Allah."[18]

Endowed with *firāsat* (intuitive ability – a blessing from Allah) the Shaykh would reprimand those whose motives were questionable or displayed performative piety in his presence. It is related that a resident who had just completed his *hajj* came to pay homage to the Shaykh. He was told by the Shaykh to repent (*tawba*), an unexpected response from him. The resident

---

[17] Abdul Kader Choughley, *Fazlur Rahman Ansari: Life and Thought* (Springs, 2012), 63-4.

[18] Cited in Malik, *The Grey Falcon,* 210.

protested that he had just returned from pilgrimage and thus all his sins were forgiven to which the Shaykh tersely replied: "I know that, but then there was fornication, sins and flagrantly corrupt behaviour!"[19] The resident thought that this was a private matter and was dumbstruck when the Shaykh revealed his immoral behaviour on *hajj*.

A word about the *Malfuzāt*[20] of the Shaykh. Unlike the *Fath ar-Rabbāni* which was compiled by his son 'Abdur Razzāq in a structured format, this slim volume has been included as an Appendix to his celebrated works. For example, there is no topical order or date and place of the Shaykh's gems of wisdom contained in this work. Presumably, the title in Arabic which is translated as *Utterances* in English has been affixed to this work. In contrast, *Fath ar-Rabbāni* is prefaced by a heading, date and place, facilitating easy reading. We have to surmise that the collection of *Malfuzāt* was recorded in an informal way at the Shaykh's residence and the *ribāt*. A helpful clue to the composition of this work is the questions posed to the Shaykh.[21] In addition, there are references to the state and behaviour of the Shaykh that has a circumstantial setting. Moreover, the style and content of *Malfuzāt* are in line with the key themes explored in *Futuh al-Ghaib* and *Fath ar-Rabbāni*.

A question was posed to the Shaykh about earning a living. He reminded the listeners that acquiring *halāl* sustenance is a means (*sabab*) to follow the *Sunnah* of the Holy Prophet (pbuh). Essentially, earning a living (*kasb*) is a *Sunnah* whereas absolute trust (*tawakkul*) is his spiritual

---

19 *Ibid.*, 215.
20 Shaikh 'Abd Al-Qādir Al-Jilāni, *Malfuzāt: Utterances of Shaikh 'Abd Al-Qādir Al-Jilāni*, 12.
21 *Ibid.*, xvi-xv.

state. In sum, detachment from the material attachment is the ideal to follow. The Shaykh states further that the *shari'ah* and knowledge *('ilm)* of a higher level are perfect guides to reach close to Allah. For the Shaykh, there is no contradiction in developing a harmonious balance between the *shari'ah* and *tariqah*.[22] Seeking the pleasure of Allah *(ridā ilāhi)* occurs over a period of time when it is nurtured with *taqwā*. The Shaykh illustrates this point with a perceptive example. A certain person wrote three hundred and sixty stories and delivered one story every day to the local prince *(amir)*. He never got tired or bored of following this routine until he received a seal of approval from the local police. Turning to his listeners, he asks a rhetorical question: "However, you devote a few days or a few short nights to making requests of Allah, then you get bored and resort to man instead. Why not remember the man who wrote all those stories (as an important lesson)?"[23]

In the hierarchy of spiritual *(ruhāni)* virtues the Shaykh reiterates the importance of carrying out the rights of the creation *(huquq al-khalq)* while observing the rights of His Creator, Allah. Always offer people good advice *(nasiha)* as a means of drawing them closer to Allah. At the same time, the Shaykh cautions his listeners (many of whom were his students and *murīds*) not to harbour any thought of gaining benefit from the creation.[24] The Shaykh signposts other virtues in the quest for moral and spiritual excellence *(ihsān)*. He exhorts his

---

[22] *Ibid.*, 19, 37.
[23] *Ibid.*, 44.
[24] *Ibid.*, 92.

listeners to guard against the pervasive influence of passion (*hawā*) which is in marked contrast to rational contemplation (*fikr*). In a similar vein, he says that mastery over the outer aspects will definitely lead to command over the inner aspects. Knowledge too "will hold your reins, to keep you tightly in control."[25] All in all, positive qualities produce equilibrium is one's life.

We now focus on the 'state and behaviour' of the Shaykh on certain occasions: his moments of silence and deep reflection tell another story. The following accounts are indicative of the powerful impact he had on his listeners. The reporter (unnamed in the compilation) says:

A man screamed during his meeting (*majlis*) and cried: "Allah!" The Shaykh then said: "You will be questioned about this. You will be called to account for it. Why did you speak? Was it ostentation (*riyā*) or hypocrisy (*nifāq*), sincerity (*ikhlās*) or blasphemy (*shirk*)? This day is a sledge-hammer. If anyone wishes to leave, he may do so, and if anyone wishes to stay, let him stay." Then he (the Shaykh) uttered a cry and many people got up and approached him, crying and weeping in repentance.

Just then, a sparrow came and settled on his head; so, he bowed his head for it. He stayed in that position, with the bird on his head and the people on the stairs of the lectern. He did not stir until one of his companions held out his hand toward it and it flew away. Then he offered a prayer of supplication.

The people were making a great commotion with their weeping, supplications and professions of repentance. He stepped down and went out immediately to the congregational mosque (*jāmi'*) of al-Rusafa, followed by a great throng of

---

²⁵ *Ibid.*, 72.

people, amid a scene of weeping, screaming and ecstasy (*wajd*) and the shedding of clothes. Then he said: "This is the end of the age. O Allah, we take refuge from the evil thereof!" When the Shaykh had stepped down from the lectern, one of his students said to him: "You were quite extreme in your admonition, and you spoke to the person very harshly!" But the Shaykh replied:" If my words had any effect on him, he will surely come back for more." (The man did, in fact, attend the meeting regularly from then. He would visit the Shaykh at other times, outside the formal session and always behaved with the utmost humility and modesty in his presence.)[26]

The Shaykh is remembered by several titles, reflecting his *tajdidi* contributions and spiritual status. Over time the Shaykh was recognised for his thorough grounding in the Islamic sciences combined with his love for humanity. It is an understatement to suggest that these were honorific titles conferred ceremoniously on him due to his amazing personality. The circumstantial settings, however, underpin his powerful efforts at regenerating the *ummah* whose impact is still felt to this day.

The epithet or title *muhyi' al-din* fits perfectly with the Shaykh's reformatory efforts. His decades-long call for the overhaul of the Muslim society in a period of political turmoil brought about an impactful revival that reached the Muslim world. One account tells of his encounter with an invalid person who appealed for assistance. As a result, his limbs were restored to their former state indicating that he was now healthy and robust. The symbolism is clear: like the decaying body, the Shaykh would revive the body politic of the *ummah* in accordance with the Qur'ān and the *Sunnah*. In the revivalist perspective, the Shaykh's contributions have been remarkable

---

[26] *Ibid.,* 116-7.

in their scope and impact.

A powerful image, the "Grey Falcon" is best described by the Shaykh in these words: "All the other birds talk, but they do not act, whereas the falcon (*al-bāz*) acts and does without talking."[27] This title by which the Shaykh is widely known is associated with his total obedience to Allah. Like the falcon which always does the bidding of the master, without question, and returns to his hand, the case of the Shaykh to his Master, Allah Almighty, is the same. A poetic verse further illustrates his unique position:

The Falcon are you, so if you should boast it would not be vain conceit ('ujb),
For other people in my eyes are turtledoves at best.

"This foot of mine is upon the neck of every saint of Allah." is the famous declaration of the Shaykh. According to al-Hafiz Abu'l 'Izz al-Baghdadi, the Shaykh was busy with his regular *majlis* in the *ribāt* in the presence of over fifty distinguished *shaykhs* of Iraq when he made this declaration. All of them bowed their heads in humility as an expression of implicit faith in the Shaykh's unique status. Another report states that this position was unprecedented in the history of *tasawwuf* as there were no saints in the past who had made such a declaration. Several interpretations suggest that the declaration had a symbolic significance as the foot signified power and authority. This implied that the Shaykh's spiritual authority was epoch-making. In other words, it was couched in metaphorical language and reminiscent of utterances made in the past by

---

[27] *Qalā'id al-Jawāhir*, 121.

the great *awliyā*.[28] In a broader context, the uniqueness of this declaration was associated with the towering personality of the Shaykh. In contrast, another interpretation stated that the Shaykh was in full awareness of this command and uttered it accordingly.[29] To what extent it is applicable to all the saints and in all times has been a subject of discussion by the scholars from the various *silsilahs* (spiritual orders).

It is an undisputed fact that no reformer with an illuminated soul was more successful than the Shaykh in bringing about a revival of the true Islamic spirit. He was the exemplar in changing the lives of the masses by enabling them to attain the stage of the reality of faith (*haqiqat al-imān*) and moral and spiritual excellence (*ihsān*).

---

[28] For example, Husayn ibn Mansur al-Hallaj who uttered the controversial statement: "*Anal Haqq: I am the Truth.*" in a state of spiritual ecstasy (*wajd*), which provoked the condemnation of the *'ulama*. He was executed for this statement.
[29] For a detailed discussion, see *Qalā'id al-Jawāhir*, 93-108.

Tafsir Jilāni: New Horizons

Tafsir Jilāni: An Overview

In recent years the discovery of *Tafsir Jilāni* has added new insights into the Shaykh's contribution to the tafsir tradition. Although this is a significant work within the mainstream sufi tafsirs, the paucity of background information to make an interpretive reading is a somewhat challenging undertaking. Needless to say, this multivolume tafsir has to be read in context of the Shaykh's multifaceted contributions to Islamic reformist thought.

Tafsir Jilāni was discovered by a direct descendant of the Shaykh, Muhammad Fadhil al-Kaylani of Turkey. There is an interesting account about this distinguished scholar's extensive years of travel in search of the Shaykh's manuscripts which were deposited in many universities of the Muslim world and the West. Of course, this tafsir was a rare find after a period of more than eight hundred years. More noteworthy were the manuscripts deposited in the libraries of the Vatican, indicating the serious study of the Shaykh's literary contributions undertaken by scholars in the field of Orientalist studies. The period 1997-2002, was a productive phase for Muhammad Fadhil in the editing of new books written by the Shaykh. In 2009 the multivolume tafsir was published in Istanbul, Turkey.

According to the Muhammad Fadhil who served as the editor, each volume of the work was written by a different interpreter and their intellectual temperament and technical skills come to the fore. Some prominent features include the Shaykh's elaboration of "Surah al-Fatiha" in a succinct, yet lucid style. In addition, there is a general theme that highlights the contents of each *surah* for the readers. It is a lesson-based approach that seeks to connect the readers with the message and teachings of the sacred text. In line with his reformist vision, the Shaykh makes pertinent mention of the virtues (*fadhā'i!*) of particular *surahs* and occasionally includes prayers (*du'ās)* from the *surah* under discussion. We must not forget the *islāhi* contents in the tafsir that are central to his presentation of the *shari'ah-tariqah* perspective.[1]

Without delving into the technicalities of the sufi tafsirs, there are a few pointers that will help the readers understand their approach to this genre. There are verses containing figurative meanings as well as mystical dimensions that have been under scrutiny by sufi scholars. This approach, in turn, gave rise to multi-layered interpretations that in many instances were at variance with the traditional tafsirs. The Qur'ān as an ocean of knowledge was interpreted in a mystical way: it implied that the accepted norms *('u!um*) were limiting and did not allow for refreshing perspectives within the *tasawwuf* tradition. In other words, tafsir could be subjective and could based on flashes of illuminations that were beyond the realm of tradition-bound analysis. This mindset saw particular verses containing ambiguous meanings (*mutashābihāt*) and given a sufi touch in which the spiritual stages are emphasised. Not surprisingly therefore, is the reading of the text with the

---

[1] Information gleaned from *Sheikh Abdul Qādir Al-Jilāni and Tafsir al-Jilāni*, (n.d.), 48-55.

presence of the heart (*hudhur al-qalb*), a practice of embodying reflection, contemplation and spiritual awareness. Again, the hierarchy of values are reinforced to approach the text in a spirit of humility. For the traditional *mufassir* (commentator) the text has essentially explicit meanings and are derived from the corpus of the *hadith* literature. For the general reader the Prophetic teachings take precedence over the hidden meanings as advocated by the sufis[2]

Classical Sufi Commentaries

We now turn to the different types of sufi tafsirs preceding *Tafsir Jilāni.* A notable mention is Sahl al-Tustari (d. 896) whose *Tafsir al-Qur'ān al-'Azim* was compiled by one of his disciples. It is not a complete tafsir but an interpretation of certain verses and their spiritual significance. A femous sufi known for his self-abstinence (*zuhd*), al-Tustari focused on the spiritual meanings of verses in the light of self-introspection (*muhāsabah).* Writing on the verse: "And in his absence the people of Musa took the effigy of a calf (made of their ornaments)," al-Tustari says that which keeps a man away from Allah is his own, golden calf. This may be his children, wealth and other worldly possessions. The only way to destroy the 'golden calf ' is to bring the (*nafs*) ego under control.[3] The sufi interpretation is self-explanatory. There are other verses too that are extremely symbolic and which are at odds with clear-cut interpretations in the authoritative tafsirs.

Abu 'Abd al-Rahman al-Sulami (d. 1021) wrote *Haqā'iq al-*

---

[2] For a detailed discussion on this aspect, see Kristin Zahra Sands, *Sufi Commentaries on the Qur'ān in Classical Islam* (New York, 2006).

[3] Rashid Ahmad Jullundhri, *Qur'anic Exegesis in Classical Literature with Particular Reference to Abu al-Qāsim al-Qushayri* (Kuala Lumpur, 2010), 66-7.

Tafsir which has been critiqued in the scholarly circles. One of the main objections to the tafsir is his reference to the heretical views of Husayn ibn Mansur al-Hallaj and his 'I am the Truth" utterance. In this Preface, al-Sulami states that it is not an original work, but a collection of the sayings of the sufis and other distinguished Islamic personalities. However, it is considered the first complete work in the sufi tafsir tradition. In addition, al-Sulami recognises the validity of the traditional and sufi tafsirs without detracting the merits of both these genres. In the strain of mystical allusion, he tends to focus too much, in fact disproportionately on symbolism relating to the detachment of this worldly life and the conquest of the lower self (*nafs*). Consider the following verse and Sulami's interpretation: "Behold, the truly virtuous will indeed be in bliss." (82: 13). Quoting Ja'far al-Sadiq he states that the word '*na'im*' is divine knowledge whereas '*jahim*' refers to carnal desires. In some instances, he combines linguistic and spiritual meanings which are relevant to the tafsir to exemplify the ego-over-everything mindset. In his estimation, it is only the sufis who appreciate the essence of the divine text largely on account of their spiritual striving (*mujāhadah*).[4]

It was the great Abu Hamid al-Ghazali (d. 111) who wrote his masterpiece *Mishkāt al-Masābih* on the verses of the light (*nur*) in Surah al-Nur (24:35). There is no doubt that this symbolic commentary carved out a niche within the traditionalist tafsir and in some way brought the sufi commentaries as an integral component to this genre.[5] The Shaykh too prefaces his *Sirr al-Asrār* (The Secret of Secrets) with a letter to the reader in which he uses captivating imagery in the light of the Surah al-Nur

---

[4] Ibid., 69-70.
[5] Ibid., 74-5.

verses. The Shaykh explains:

> When the light from *Allah* (Who) *is the light of the heavens and the earth* ... begins to shine upon the regions of your heart, the lamp of the heart will be lit. The lamp of the heart *is in a glass, the glass as it were a brightly shining star.* Then within that heart, the lightning shaft of divine discoveries strikes. This lightning shaft will emanate from the thunderclouds of meaning *neither of the East nor of the West, lit from a blessed olive tree* ... and throw light upon the tree of discovery, so pure, so transparent that it *sheds light though fire does not touch it.* Then the lamp of wisdom is lit by itself. How can it remain unlit when the light of Allah's secrets shines over it?[6]

In Chapter 4 mention is made of al-Qushayri's celebrated work *Risāla* and its realignment of sufi literature within the ambit of the *shari'ah* and *tariqah*. Of special significance is his mystical commentary *Latā'if al-Ishārāt,* a treasure house of profound thought, "reflecting his mastery of the literary, exegetical, theological and juridical discourses."[7] In other words, the tafsir is a fusion of traditional sufi interpretation. However, the primary goal of al-Qushayri is to provide guidance for the spiritual aspirants (*murīds*), those who seek deeper knowledge and intimacy with Allah. In particular *Latā'if al-Ishārāt* is a compilation of the transmitted wisdom of the earlier sufis and al-Qushayri's deep study of the Qur'ān. Although the words 'sufi' and '*tasawwuf*' rarely appear in the commentary there

---

[6] *The Secret of Secrets,* xlvii. The italicised text is the translation of the Qur'ānic verse.

[7] Qushayri, *Latā'if al-Ishārāt: Subtle Allusions.* Translated by Kristin Zahra Sands (Louisville, 2017), 7.

are strong markers of the mystical dimensions found in his interpretation of the Qur'ānic verses. Overall, al-Qushayri criticises the formalism of the 'ulama whereas his presentation of the Qur'ānic verses is devoid of the complex sufi concepts that have no bearing to the Prophetic teachings. In his view, the inner meanings have mystical dimensions and can be assimilated within the *shari'ah* tradition. The following comment is illustrative of this synthesis:

> Al-Qushayri emphasises the spiritual aspect of the Qur'ānic teaching when it serves the purpose of the Qur'ānic exegesis. Al-Qushayri was a practical man and wanted his fellow men to be sincere in their ideas, intoxicated with divine love and completely free from the bondage of matter and self.[8]

Before we attempt to examine *Tafsir Jilāni* a few points need to be kept in mind to appreciate the Shaykh's contributions to this genre. An introductory comment on the *tafsir ishāri* will be helpful to contextualise his holistic interpretation of the divine text. *Tafsir Ishāri* focuses on the mystical dimensions of verses which do not necessarily have *mutashābihāt* (allegorical) significance. As we have seen in this chapter, the sufi-commentator relies on his spiritual intuition or experience which is largely influenced by the category of states (*ahwāl*) found in the *tasawwuf* tradition. The decoding of the hidden meanings of the verses has lent serious debates among the traditional *mufassirs*[9] about the validity of this approach.

A closer study of the *Ghunya li Tālibi* reveals the Shaykh's

---

[8] Jullundhri, *Qur'anic Exegesis in Classical Literature*, 138.
[9] A *mufassir* is a commentator (exegete) of the Qur'ān.

wide breadth of knowledge of tafsir. He goes beyond the standard interpretation of the verses giving numerous explanations, sometimes to a single verse. His mastery over the early tafsirs like Ibn 'Abbas, al-Suddi, etc. is impressive. The Shaykh expands on these interpretation by including the citations from the *Sahābah*, pious predecessors (*salaf*) and influential sufi personalities. By way of example, the Shaykh gives the exegesis (*tafsir*) of the first few verses of Surah al-Fajr (89) from the interpretations of the *Sahābah* and the multivolume *Tafsir al-Tabari*.[10] In his other works his grounding in the tafsir literature is vividly brought out.

There are several distinctive features of *Tafsir Jilāni* which are indicative of the Shaykh's creative approach to this tradition. The Shaykh has explicated numerous meanings for *basmallah* in *Ghunya li Tālibi* as a reference point to his vast learning in the various Islamic subjects. Furthermore, in his tafsir he skillfully prefaces each surah with a brilliant explanation of the phrase: "In the name of Allah, Most Gracious, Most Merciful". It covers a wide range of meanings related to *'aqidah* (belief), teachings and practice while highlighting the sublime message of Allah's attributes of mercy and compassion to mankind. The Shaykh extends these meanings in expressive language and prepares the readers to connect to the divine text in a spirit of reverence and humility. Allah's attributes are comprehensive and include all the other divine names (*asmā'al-husnā*) on which the phenomena of the universe are based. At the same time, the readers experience a spiritual affinity as they ponder, contemplate and reflect upon Allah's majesty and reaffirm *tawhīd* and total trust (*tawakkul*) in order to earn His pleasure.

---

[10] Cited in Malik, *The Grey Falcon*, 158. For a detailed discussion of the *tafsir* see, Al-Tabari. *The Commentary on the Qur'ān*. vol. 1. (Oxford, 1990), ix-xlii.

The 'tree of faith' as the Shaykh aptly describes in one of his discourses, has inner resources and potentials leading the believers to develop an abiding conviction (*yaqin*) with their Lord and this trait ties up in many ways with the essence of *basmallah*.[11]

Surah al-Fātiha

A brief analysis of Surah al-Fatiha reveals gems of meaning and wisdom in *Tafsir Jilāni*. It also provides a lucid explanation about the significance of the surah.

Al-hamdu in its literal sense refers to praise. The Shaykh elaborates on this term to cover all possible shades of meaning associated with *hamd*. It emanates from men who are constantly praising their Creator in a spirit of obedience. Moreover, they express unconditionally and consistently their gratitude to their Benefactor. *Li'llāhi*, according to the Shaykh, should reflect praises to Allah whose attributes are all-encompassing to the worlds and what they contain. *Rabb 'il 'ālamin* expresses Allah's nurturing and training for His creation in both worlds, without which the universe will cease to exist.

The interpretation of the first verse of the surah by the Shaykh is intended to illustrate his approach to tafsir. The multi-layered meanings are indicative of the Shaykh's absorption in the 'oceans of divine knowledge.' What is striking in the explanation is the way he articulates, albeit briefly, the attributes of Allah. In his major writings there is a detailed discussion on the attributes of Allah and its relation to man and the universe.

---

[11] *Futuh al-Ghaib*, 63-4.

The gist of the remaining verses of Surah al-Fatiha is now given. Allah is the Master of the Day of Reckoning which is named as the Day of Resurrection "in which the earth is crushed and the first and last records in the earth are folded up." The veils and curtains are removed and nothing remains except Allah. The *'abd* (servant) is confirmed in his position in the Afterlife due to his complete obedience to Allah and therefore he is entitled to converse with his Lord without any curtain and barrier.

There is direct link between the servant and his Creator: he worships Allah as there is none other in existence except Him. His *'ibādah* mirrors a sense of humility and submission because there is no object of worship and goal to reach for except Allah. In the same vein, Allah's help is not determined by the level of one's *'ibādah*; rather, man's helplessness requires Allah's help at all times because there is no recourse except Him.

Guidance (*hidāyat*) implies earning Allah's kindness and graciousness in the pursuit of the straight path with the sole purpose of "reaching the summit of *tawhīd*." The path of those whom Allah has blessed are the Prophets, the champions of truth, the martyrs and the righteous and upright people who will be his companions.

Those who earn Allah's wrath are the hesitators, the doubters and those whose minds are filled with illusions about the straight path. Likewise, the reasons for those who go astray are "delusions of this base world and the enticements of the devils (*shayātin*) from the road of the truth and the way of certainty."

Another salient feature of *Tafsir Jilāni* is the concluding message (*khātima*) of each surah. In the case of surah al-Fatiha, the message has a deeper symbolic meaning. The seven verses of the surah correspond to the seven heavens and the seven cosmic stars and contain essential divine attributes. Contemplation of these phenomena will strengthen one's level of *tawhīd*. In contrast, there are seven 'infernal valleys' that have destructive tendencies and are counterproductive to one's spiritual growth. It is only the Muhammadan path (*tariqah*) as described in the Qur'ān that is to be followed for the overall development of one's personality which is pleasing to Allah.[12]

Surah al-Baqarah

A brief overview of the tafsir of surah al-Baqarah reveals important facets of the Shaykh's methodology. Symbolic significance (*ishārī*) and literal meaning (*lafzī*) are given appropriate attention in view of his *shari'ah-tariqah* approach. Framed from a different perspective, the outer (*zāhir*) and inner (*bātin*) aspects are meant to give a well-developed presentation of the key themes in the surah. This is more relevant when one considers the *asbāb al-nuzul* (reasons for revelation), the *ahkām* (shari'ah prescriptions) in this Madinan surah. How does the

Shaykh approach its comprehensiveness is best illustrated by the following examples:

The Shaykh alludes to the content of the surah in the form of a hierarchy: *shari'ah*, ethics and *tawhīd*. In the broader sense, the surah includes stories of the Prophets and similes (*tamthil*), reinforcing the universal message and teachings of Islam. In the case of the Shaykh's interpretation of these verses, he does not provide detailed discussion about the relevant

---

[12] Summarised from *Tafsir Jilāni*. vol.1 (Istanbul, n.d.),

asbāb al-nuzul nor does he delve into the niceties of vocabulary. Brevity informs his explanation of the words and phrases to the verses under discussion. For example, verse 238 in the surah mentions midday prayer. It is a unanimous view by the classical commentators that it refers to the 'Asr prayer. However, the Shaykh offers a somewhat different meaning in respect of the affinity between two people on a spiritual level. This explanation must be understood in the context of the traditional meanings also given by him. Likewise, for the Shaykh, the Arabic word *barq* (lightning) in verse 19 is closely associated with spiritual illumination and its effects on the soul. Without disregarding the literal meaning the Shaykh adds a new dimension to the word by suggesting that the *nur* (light) *of imān* is contrasted with the lightning that envelops the heart of the hypocrites. The verses relating to the heavens and the earth are also explained metaphorically by the Shaykh. In the strain of *tawhīd*, the Shaykh explains that the heavens are essentially the attributes of Allah that are manifested in the universe and creation. The earth represents humility while night symbolises darkness, blindness and ignorance. It is contrasted with day which symbolises the divine presence.[13]

Tafsir Studies and the Shaykh

Tafsir embraces the vast corpus of *hadith* literature and the Shaykh, too, demonstrates his mastery over this subject. He cites the six authentic *hadith* compilations to support his explanation of the verses. In some instances, the gist of the

---

[13] For a detailed analysis of Surah al-Baqarah in *Tafsir Jilāni*, see Miftakhul Huda, *The Method and Style of the Interpretation of Syeikh Abdul Qādir Al-Jilāni in Tafsir Jilāni* (Semarang, 2013), 63-75.

hadith is only given and the editor adds the necessary details in the footnote. It must not be forgotten that the manuscript was found approximately eight hundred years after the Shaykh's death, thus requiring the painstaking editing process of collating, systematising and giving technical shape to it. However, it has added fresh perspectives about the Shaykh's status in the field of the *tafsir* genre. Elsewhere in the study mention is made of the Shaykh's vast knowledge of the *tafsir* corpus. The following incident underscores his mastery of and insight into its spiritual meanings.

Hafiz Abu'l 'Abbās narrates that Shaykh Jamaluddin ibn al-Jawzi, a noted scholar in *hadith* and tafsir literature accompanied him to one of the *majlis* of the Shaykh. As the Shaykh discussed one possible interpretation of the verse, the narrator turned to ibn Jawzi and asked him if he was familiar with it to which he replied in the affirmative. This response occurred several times.

"Then the Shaykh referred to yet another interpretation, so I asked Shaykh Jamaluddin: 'Are you familiar with this one?' This time his answer was: 'No, I am not acquainted with this one.' He gave me an equally negative response to each of my subsequent questions, as the Shaykh went on to mention yet another interpretation, followed by yet another, until he reached a grand total of forty different ways of understanding that same Qur'ānic verse. Shaykh Jamaluddin was utterly astonished, as he marvelled at the vast scope of knowledge demonstrated by our master, Shaykh 'Abd al-Qādir (may Allah be well pleased with him).

Finally, the Shaykh (turning to both of them) said: "Let us have done with the talk (*qāl*), and now let us return to the spiritual state (*hāl*)."[14]

---

[14] *Qalā'id al-Jawāhir*, 158.

In sum, *Tafsir Jilāni* has not received the attention in the scholarly circles as it richly deserves. In fact, it is an understudied multivolume work that is no less in importance than other classical *tafsirs*. On a positive note, there is a growing interest among the Indonesian scholars in particular to undertake a critical study of the Shaykh's significant contribution to the *tafsir* tradition.

Tafsir Jilāni: New Horizons

Tafsir Jilāni: An Overview

In recent years the discovery of *Tafsir Jilāni* has added new insights into the Shaykh's contribution to the tafsir tradition. Although this is a significant work within the mainstream sufi tafsirs, the paucity of background information to make an interpretive reading is a somewhat challenging undertaking. Needless to say, this multivolume tafsir has to be read in context of the Shaykh's multifaceted contributions to Islamic reformist thought.

Tafsir Jilāni was discovered by a direct descendant of the Shaykh, Muhammad Fadhil al-Kaylani of Turkey. There is an interesting account about this distinguished scholar's extensive years of travel in search of the Shaykh's manuscripts which were deposited in many universities of the Muslim world and the West. Of course, this tafsir was a rare find after a period of more than eight hundred years. More noteworthy were the manuscripts deposited in the libraries of the Vatican, indicating the serious study of the Shaykh's literary contributions undertaken by scholars in the field of Orientalist studies. The period 1997-2002, was a productive phase for Muhammad Fadhil in the editing of new books written by the Shaykh. In 2009 the multivolume tafsir was published in Istanbul, Turkey.

According to the Muhammad Fadhil who served as the editor, each volume of the work was written by a different interpreter and their intellectual temperament and technical skills come to the fore. Some prominent features include the Shaykh's elaboration of "Surah al-Fatiha" in a succinct, yet lucid style. In addition, there is a general theme that highlights the contents of each *surah* for the readers. It is a lesson-based approach that seeks to connect the readers with the message and teachings of the sacred text. In line with his reformist vision, the Shaykh makes pertinent mention of the virtues (*fadhā'il*) of particular *surahs* and occasionally includes prayers (*du'ās*) from the *surah* under discussion. We must not forget the *islāhi* contents in the tafsir that are central to his presentation of the *shari'ah-tariqah* perspective.[1]

Without delving into the technicalities of the sufi tafsirs, there are a few pointers that will help the readers understand their approach to this genre. There are verses containing figurative meanings as well as mystical dimensions that have been under scrutiny by sufi scholars. This approach, in turn, gave rise to multi-layered interpretations that in many instances were at variance with the traditional tafsirs. The Qur'ān as an ocean of knowledge was interpreted in a mystical way: it implied that the accepted norms *('ulum)* were limiting and did not allow for refreshing perspectives within the *tasawwuf* tradition. In other words, tafsir could be subjective and could based on flashes of illuminations that were beyond the realm of tradition-bound analysis. This mindset saw particular verses containing ambiguous meanings (*mutashābihāt*) and given a sufi touch in which the spiritual stages are emphasised. Not surprisingly therefore, is the reading of the text with the

---

[1] Information gleaned from *Sheikh Abdul Qādir Al-Jilāni and Tafsir al-Jilāni*, (n.d.), 48-55.

presence of the heart (*hudhur al-qalb*), a practice of embodying reflection, contemplation and spiritual awareness. Again, the hierarchy of values are reinforced to approach the text in a spirit of humility. For the traditional *mufassir* (commentator) the text has essentially explicit meanings and are derived from the corpus of the *hadith* literature. For the general reader the Prophetic teachings take precedence over the hidden meanings as advocated by the sufis[2]

Classical Sufi Commentaries

We now turn to the different types of sufi tafsirs preceding *Tafsir Jilānī*. A notable mention is Sahl al-Tustari (d. 896) whose *Tafsir al-Qur'ān al-'Azim* was compiled by one of his disciples. It is not a complete tafsir but an interpretation of certain verses and their spiritual significance. A femous sufi known for his self-abstinence (*zuhd*), al-Tustari focused on the spiritual meanings of verses in the light of self-introspection (*muhāsabah)*. Writing on the verse: "And in his absence the people of Musa took the effigy of a calf (made of their ornaments)," al-Tustari says that which keeps a man away from Allah is his own, golden calf. This may be his children, wealth and other worldly possessions. The only way to destroy the 'golden calf' is to bring the (*nafs*) ego under control.[3] The sufi interpretation is self-explanatory. There are other verses too that are extremely symbolic and which are at odds with clear-cut interpretations in the authoritative tafsirs.

Abu 'Abd al-Rahman al-Sulami (d. 1021) wrote *Haqā'iq al-*

---

[2] For a detailed discussion on this aspect, see Kristin Zahra Sands, *Sufi Commentaries on the Qur'ān in Classical Islam* (New York, 2006).

[3] Rashid Ahmad Jullundhri, *Qur'anic Exegesis in Classical Literature with Particular Reference to Abu al-Qāsim al-Qushayri* (Kuala Lumpur, 2010), 66-7.

Tafsir which has been critiqued in the scholarly circles. One of the main objections to the tafsir is his reference to the heretical views of Husayn ibn Mansur al-Hallaj and his 'I am the Truth" utterance. In this Preface, al-Sulami states that it is not an original work, but a collection of the sayings of the sufis and other distinguished Islamic personalities. However, it is considered the first complete work in the sufi tafsir tradition. In addition, al-Sulami recognises the validity of the traditional and sufi tafsirs without detracting the merits of both these genres. In the strain of mystical allusion, he tends to focus too much, in fact disproportionately on symbolism relating to the detachment of this worldly life and the conquest of the lower self (*nafs*). Consider the following verse and Sulami's interpretation: "Behold, the truly virtuous will indeed be in bliss." (82: 13). Quoting Ja'far al-Sadiq he states that the word 'na'im' is divine knowledge whereas '*jahim*' refers to carnal desires. In some instances, he combines linguistic and spiritual meanings which are relevant to the tafsir to exemplify the ego-over-everything mindset. In his estimation, it is only the sufis who appreciate the essence of the divine text largely on account of their spiritual striving (*mujāhadah*).[4]

It was the great Abu Hamid al-Ghazali (d. 111) who wrote his masterpiece *Mishkāt al-Masābih* on the verses of the light (*nur*) in Surah al-Nur (24:35). There is no doubt that this symbolic commentary carved out a niche within the traditionalist tafsir and in some way brought the sufi commentaries as an integral component to this genre.[5] The Shaykh too prefaces his *Sirr al-Asrār* (The Secret of Secrets) with a letter to the reader in which he uses captivating imagery in the light of the Surah al-Nur

---

[4] Ibid., 69-70.
[5] Ibid., 74-5.

verses. The Shaykh explains:

> When the light from *Allah* (Who) *is the light of the heavens and the earth* ... begins to shine upon the regions of your heart, the lamp of the heart will be lit. The lamp of the heart *is in a glass, the glass as it were a brightly shining star*. Then within that heart, the lightning shaft of divine discoveries strikes. This lightning shaft will emanate from the thunderclouds of meaning *neither of the East nor of the West, lit from a blessed olive tree* ... and throw light upon the tree of discovery, so pure, so transparent that it *sheds light though fire does not touch it*. Then the lamp of wisdom is lit by itself. How can it remain unlit when the light of Allah's secrets shines over it?[6]

In Chapter 4 mention is made of al-Qushayri's celebrated work *Risāla* and its realignment of sufi literature within the ambit of the *shari'ah* and *tariqah*. Of special significance is his mystical commentary *Latā'if al-Ishārāt*, a treasure house of profound thought, "reflecting his mastery of the literary, exegetical, theological and juridical discourses."[7] In other words, the tafsir is a fusion of traditional sufi interpretation. However, the primary goal of al-Qushayri is to provide guidance for the spiritual aspirants (*murīds*), those who seek deeper knowledge and intimacy with Allah. In particular *Latā'if al-Ishārāt* is a compilation of the transmitted wisdom of the earlier sufis and al-Qushayri's deep study of the Qur'ān. Although the words 'sufi' and '*tasawwuf*' rarely appear in the commentary there

---

[6] *The Secret of Secrets*, xlvii. The italicised text is the translation of the Qur'ānic verse.

[7] Qushayri, *Latā'if al-Ishārāt: Subtle Allusions*. Translated by Kristin Zahra Sands (Louisville, 2017), 7.

are strong markers of the mystical dimensions found in his interpretation of the Qur'ānic verses. Overall, al-Qushayri criticises the formalism of the 'ulama whereas his presentation of the Qur'ānic verses is devoid of the complex sufi concepts that have no bearing to the Prophetic teachings. In his view, the inner meanings have mystical dimensions and can be assimilated within the *shari'ah* tradition. The following comment is illustrative of this synthesis:

> Al-Qushayri emphasises the spiritual aspect of the Qur'ānic teaching when it serves the purpose of the Qur'ānic exegesis. Al-Qushayri was a practical man and wanted his fellow men to be sincere in their ideas, intoxicated with divine love and completely free from the bondage of matter and self.[8]

Before we attempt to examine *Tafsir Jilāni* a few points need to be kept in mind to appreciate the Shaykh's contributions to this genre. An introductory comment on the *tafsir ishāri* will be helpful to contextualise his holistic interpretation of the divine text. *Tafsir Ishāri* focuses on the mystical dimensions of verses which do not necessarily have *mutashābihāt* (allegorical) significance. As we have seen in this chapter, the sufi-commentator relies on his spiritual intuition or experience which is largely influenced by the category of states (*ahwāl*) found in the *tasawwuf* tradition. The decoding of the hidden meanings of the verses has lent serious debates among the traditional *mufassirs*[9] about the validity of this approach.

A closer study of the *Ghunya li Tālibi* reveals the Shaykh's

---

[8] Jullundhri, *Qur'anic Exegesis in Classical Literature*, 138.
[9] A *mufassir* is a commentator (exegete) of the Qur'ān.

wide breadth of knowledge of tafsir. He goes beyond the standard interpretation of the verses giving numerous explanations, sometimes to a single verse. His mastery over the early tafsirs like Ibn 'Abbas, al-Suddi, etc. is impressive. The Shaykh expands on these interpretation by including the citations from the *Sahābah*, pious predecessors (*salaf*) and influential sufi personalities. By way of example, the Shaykh gives the exegesis (*tafsir*) of the first few verses of Surah al-Fajr (89) from the interpretations of the *Sahābah* and the multivolume *Tafsir al-Tabari*.[10] In his other works his grounding in the tafsir literature is vividly brought out.

There are several distinctive features of *Tafsir Jilāni* which are indicative of the Shaykh's creative approach to this tradition. The Shaykh has explicated numerous meanings for *basmallah* in *Ghunya li Tālibi* as a reference point to his vast learning in the various Islamic subjects. Furthermore, in his tafsir he skillfully prefaces each surah with a brilliant explanation of the phrase: "In the name of Allah, Most Gracious, Most Merciful". It covers a wide range of meanings related to *'aqidah* (belief), teachings and practice while highlighting the sublime message of Allah's attributes of mercy and compassion to mankind. The Shaykh extends these meanings in expressive language and prepares the readers to connect to the divine text in a spirit of reverence and humility. Allah's attributes are comprehensive and include all the other divine names (*asmā'al-husnā*) on which the phenomena of the universe are based. At the same time, the readers experience a spiritual affinity as they ponder, contemplate and reflect upon Allah's majesty and reaffirm *tawhīd* and total trust (*tawakkul*) in order to earn His pleasure.

---

[10] Cited in Malik, *The Grey Falcon*, 158. For a detailed discussion of the *tafsir* see, Al-Tabari. *The Commentary on the Qur'ān*. vol. 1. (Oxford, 1990), ix-xlii.

The 'tree of faith' as the Shaykh aptly describes in one of his discourses, has inner resources and potentials leading the believers to develop an abiding conviction (*yaqin*) with their Lord and this trait ties up in many ways with the essence of *basmallah*.[11]

Surah al-Fātiha

A brief analysis of Surah al-Fatiha reveals gems of meaning and wisdom in *Tafsir Jilāni*. It also provides a lucid explanation about the significance of the surah.

Al-hamdu in its literal sense refers to praise. The Shaykh elaborates on this term to cover all possible shades of meaning associated with *hamd*. It emanates from men who are constantly praising their Creator in a spirit of obedience. Moreover, they express unconditionally and consistently their gratitude to their Benefactor. *Li'llāhi*, according to the Shaykh, should reflect praises to Allah whose attributes are all-encompassing to the worlds and what they contain. *Rabb 'il 'ālamin* expresses Allah's nurturing and training for His creation in both worlds, without which the universe will cease to exist.

The interpretation of the first verse of the surah by the Shaykh is intended to illustrate his approach to tafsir. The multi-layered meanings are indicative of the Shaykh's absorption in the 'oceans of divine knowledge.' What is striking in the explanation is the way he articulates, albeit briefly, the attributes of Allah. In his major writings there is a detailed discussion on the attributes of Allah and its relation to man and the universe.

---

[11] *Futuh al-Ghaib*, 63-4.

The gist of the remaining verses of Surah al-Fatiha is now given. Allah is the Master of the Day of Reckoning which is named as the Day of Resurrection "in which the earth is crushed and the first and last records in the earth are folded up." The veils and curtains are removed and nothing remains except Allah. The *'abd* (servant) is confirmed in his position in the Afterlife due to his complete obedience to Allah and therefore he is entitled to converse with his Lord without any curtain and barrier.

There is direct link between the servant and his Creator: he worships Allah as there is none other in existence except Him. His *'ibādah* mirrors a sense of humility and submission because there is no object of worship and goal to reach for except Allah. In the same vein, Allah's help is not determined by the level of one's *'ibādah*; rather, man's helplessness requires Allah's help at all times because there is no recourse except Him.

Guidance (*hidāyat*) implies earning Allah's kindness and graciousness in the pursuit of the straight path with the sole purpose of "reaching the summit of *tawhīd*." The path of those whom Allah has blessed are the Prophets, the champions of truth, the martyrs and the righteous and upright people who will be his companions.

Those who earn Allah's wrath are the hesitators, the doubters and those whose minds are filled with illusions about the straight path. Likewise, the reasons for those who go astray are "delusions of this base world and the enticements of the devils (*shayātin*) from the road of the truth and the way of certainty."

Another salient feature of *Tafsir Jilāni* is the concluding message (*khātima*) of each surah. In the case of surah al-Fatiha, the message has a deeper symbolic meaning. The seven verses of the surah correspond to the seven heavens and the seven cosmic stars and contain essential divine attributes. Contemplation of these phenomena will strengthen one's level of *tawhīd*. In contrast, there are seven 'infernal valleys' that have destructive tendencies and are counterproductive to one's spiritual growth. It is only the Muhammadan path (*tariqah)* as described in the Qur'ān that is to be followed for the overall development of one's personality which is pleasing to Allah.[12]

Surah al-Baqarah

A brief overview of the tafsir of surah al-Baqarah reveals important facets of the Shaykh's methodology. Symbolic significance (*ishārī*) and literal meaning (*lafzī*) are given appropriate attention in view of his *shari'ah-tariqah* approach. Framed from a different perspective, the outer (*zāhir*) and inner (*bātin*) aspects are meant to give a well-developed presentation of the key themes in the surah. This is more relevant when one considers the *asbāb al-nuzul* (reasons for revelation), the *ahkām* (shari'ah prescriptions) in this Madinan surah. How does the

Shaykh approach its comprehensiveness is best illustrated by the following examples:

The Shaykh alludes to the content of the surah in the form of a hierarchy: *shari'ah*, ethics and *tawhīd*. In the broader sense, the surah includes stories of the Prophets and similes (*tamthil*), reinforcing the universal message and teachings of Islam. In the case of the Shaykh's interpretation of these verses, he does not provide detailed discussion about the relevant

---

[12] Summarised from *Tafsir Jilāni*. vol.1 (Istanbul, n.d.),

asbāb al-nuzul nor does he delve into the niceties of vocabulary. Brevity informs his explanation of the words and phrases to the verses under discussion. For example, verse 238 in the surah mentions midday prayer. It is a unanimous view by the classical commentators that it refers to the 'Asr prayer. However, the Shaykh offers a somewhat different meaning in respect of the affinity between two people on a spiritual level. This explanation must be understood in the context of the traditional meanings also given by him. Likewise, for the Shaykh, the Arabic word *barq* (lightning) in verse 19 is closely associated with spiritual illumination and its effects on the soul. Without disregarding the literal meaning the Shaykh adds a new dimension to the word by suggesting that the *nur* (light) *of imān* is contrasted with the lightning that envelops the heart of the hypocrites. The verses relating to the heavens and the earth are also explained metaphorically by the Shaykh. In the strain of *tawhīd*, the Shaykh explains that the heavens are essentially the attributes of Allah that are manifested in the universe and creation. The earth represents humility while night symbolises darkness, blindness and ignorance. It is contrasted with day which symbolises the divine presence.[13]

Tafsir Studies and the Shaykh

Tafsir embraces the vast corpus of *hadith* literature and the Shaykh, too, demonstrates his mastery over this subject. He cites the six authentic *hadith* compilations to support his explanation of the verses. In some instances, the gist of the

---

[13] For a detailed analysis of Surah al-Baqarah in *Tafsir Jilāni*, see Miftakhul Huda, *The Method and Style of the Interpretation of Syeikh Abdul Qādir Al-Jilāni in Tafsir Jilāni* (Semarang, 2013), 63-75.

hadith is only given and the editor adds the necessary details in the footnote. It must not be forgotten that the manuscript was found approximately eight hundred years after the Shaykh's death, thus requiring the painstaking editing process of collating, systematising and giving technical shape to it. However, it has added fresh perspectives about the Shaykh's status in the field of the *tafsir* genre. Elsewhere in the study mention is made of the Shaykh's vast knowledge of the *tafsir* corpus. The following incident underscores his mastery of and insight into its spiritual meanings.

Hafiz Abu'l 'Abbās narrates that Shaykh Jamaluddin ibn al-Jawzi, a noted scholar in *hadith* and tafsir literature accompanied him to one of the *majlis* of the Shaykh. As the Shaykh discussed one possible interpretation of the verse, the narrator turned to ibn Jawzi and asked him if he was familiar with it to which he replied in the affirmative. This response occurred several times.

"Then the Shaykh referred to yet another interpretation, so I asked Shaykh Jamaluddin: 'Are you familiar with this one?' This time his answer was: 'No, I am not acquainted with this one.' He gave me an equally negative response to each of my subsequent questions, as the Shaykh went on to mention yet another interpretation, followed by yet another, until he reached a grand total of forty different ways of understanding that same Qur'ānic verse. Shaykh Jamaluddin was utterly astonished, as he marvelled at the vast scope of knowledge demonstrated by our master, Shaykh 'Abd al-Qādir (may Allah be well pleased with him).

Finally, the Shaykh (turning to both of them) said: "Let us have done with the talk (*qāl),* and now let us return to the spiritual state (*hāl*)."[14]

---

[14] *Qalā'id al-Jawāhir,* 158.

In sum, *Tafsir Jilāni* has not received the attention in the scholarly circles as it richly deserves. In fact, it is an understudied multivolume work that is no less in importance than other classical *tafsirs*. On a positive note, there is a growing interest among the Indonesian scholars in particular to undertake a critical study of the Shaykh's significant contribution to the *tafsir* tradition.

CHAPTER EIGHT

Inner Dimensions of *Tasawwuf*

This chapter aims to identify the elementary aspects of *tasawwuf* as elaborated by the Shaykh in his major writings. A basic understanding of the inner dimensions of Islam, which are generally associated with this tradition is important to highlight the theme of the *shari'ah-tariqah* synthesis. It must be kept in mind that the path or *tariqah* has relevance in the history of *tasawwuf* and, therefore, requires elaboration in the light of the Shaykh's contributions in this field.

The tradition of *tasawwuf* has its roots in several Qur'anic verses and the *ahādith* literature. As a cognate term it refers to the process through which a permanent change in character and state takes place at both personal and social levels. In this process of change certain characteristics, attributes and temperaments are internalised in order to develop a spiritual culture. For the Shaykh the primary goal is the elimination of the bad traits of the *nafs* (self) which is consumed by worldly attachments and other distractions. This detachment is a rigorous and focused spiritual striving and is meant to lead to the single goal: Allah. There is a point in his life when the veils of Allah's *'azma* (grandeur) and *jalāl* (majesty) are revealed to him causing him to work tirelessly to the extinction of his self. In the sufi parlance it is called *fanā* and describes the state when he is physically in contact with people, but his action and movement are guided by the will of Allah. The Qur'anic verse, "He takes them out of the darkness into the light", is an appropriate description of his spiritual state. The following *hadith* reinforces this sublime level:

My servant does not draw near to me only by carrying out my obligatory duties (*farā'id*), but also draws near to me through optional acts (*nawāfil)* until I love him; and when I love him, I become his hearing, his sight, his tongue, his hand, his foot and his heart; so, through Me he hears and through Me he sees and through Me he speaks and through Me he comprehends and through Me he strikes.[1]

The Shaykh outlines certain prerequisites for the aspirant (*sālik*) to enter the fold of *tasawwuf.* To begin with he must have the correct '*aqidah* (belief) which is according to the Qur'an and the *Sunnah*. Strict adherence means that he must follow the injunctions of the *shari'ah* on two essential principles: *sidq* (truthfulness) and *ijtihād*. The aspirant must make informed decisions that do not violate the injunctions of the *shari'ah* while seeking for a leader (*qā'id*) to lead him with confidence to the spiritual path by monitoring the highs and lows of the *nafs*. In the same spirit, he should look for a companion (*mu'nis)* who is at a similar stage and who will direct the focus of the aspirant[2] on matters of the hearts, while creating an appropriate ambience to reach the final goal. The Shaykh reiterates his advice to the aspirant: find a place or refuge (*ribāt)* to steer away from worldly distractions and interacting with people whose behaviour is a barrier to the sufi path. An indispensable prerequisite for the aspirant is the spirit of generosity: to give freely while not expecting anything from anyone. In addition, the sufi path is strewn with many hurdles in the form of humiliation, hunger

---

[1] Sahih al-Bukhari, 6502.
[2] The term aspirant, seeker and *murīd* are interchangeably used in the study.

and criticism, but these must be willingly accepted for the purpose of spiritual growth, which leads to Allah's gracious favour on the aspirant's life and endearing himself to the saints *(awliyā)*.[3]

In our previous discussion (Chapter 4), the importance of a shaykh was highlighted. Although the Shaykh does not set out clear guidelines or criteria for the selection of a *shaykh*, his emphasis is on compatibility. The aspirant must choose the best *shaykh* in the area, district or region, otherwise there is a possibility that the former will be plagued by regret and doubt about the competence of his *shaykh*. In the final analysis, this will be a counterproductive relationship that can only breed doubt, scepticism and mistrust. One point comes out clearly about the *shaykh's* behaviour toward his aspirant: the nurturing element. The learning process must be phased in according to the capability of the aspirant. He should be discouraged from following his natural impulses as they have the potential to hamper his spiritual progress. Instead, he should follow the dispensations *(rukhās)* of the *shari'ah* in the easiest form available. Like a physician he should monitor the dosage of the dispensations administered over time when he sees that the aspirant is able to control his natural impulses. Gradually, the aspirant should be made to follow the stricter application of the *shari'ah* (*'azima*), one at a time so that his nature is brought into line with these prescriptions. The training under the *shaykh* will be based on the evaluation of the aspirant's spiritual needs. The process varies according to his temperament and response to the shaykh's guidance. Once the training is complete, he reaches

---

[3] An Appendix has been added to *Qala'id al-Jawāhir* with relevant excerpts compiled by the translator, Muhtar Holland. This chapter relies on the Appendix from the *Ghunya li 'Tālibi*.

Allah (*ma'rifah*) through which other veils are removed from him. In this stage he will no longer be reliant on a *shaykh*.[4]

In the Shaykh's worldview the culture of *adab* by the aspirant is paramount. Apart from the reverential behaviour to be showed to the *shaykh*, the aspirant must on no account voice his opinions randomly. Any question raised in the assembly (*majlis*) requires silence as a marker of respect. He should desist from expressing his point of view and firmly believe that his *shaykh's* answer is most appropriate on the matters raised. Overall, submission and total obedience to the *shaykh* has a healing effect for the aspirant as it removes the toxic elements that have accumulated around his *nafs*.[5]

Foundations of the Path

There are several meanings associated with the Arabic term *tariqah*. Generally, it is used for a sufi order which came into vogue after the Shaykh who is the eponymous founder of the *Qādiriyyah* order. It does have variant meanings like 'the path' or 'the method and way' depending on the context of its usage. In some instances, it is translated as brotherhood or fellowship to highlight the formation of a particular sufi order. Needless to say, these shades of meaning lend vibrancy and diversity to the *tasawwuf* tradition. There is no evidence in the Shaykh's major writings to suggest that there existed a distinct *tariqah*; so, it is safe to assume that the path was envisaged to be the teachings, counsels and guidance of the Shaykh. In the same vein, the *adhkār* [6] and *du'ās* prescribed by him for his *murids* also

---

[4] For a detailed discussion on this aspect see *Ghunya li- Tālibi*, 605-10.
[5] See Malik, *The Grey Falcon*, 173-4.
[6] *Adhkār* (sing. *dhikr*) refers to the remembrance of Allah.

indicate that his *tariqah* was taking shape during his lifetime. Framed from this perspective, the seven virtues or characteristics (*khisāl*) represent the foundations of this path.

Mujāhada

There is a constant struggle between the base desires of one's soul and the natural impulses that build unwholesome tendencies. In this context, *mujāhada* (struggle or striving) is imperative to oppose *hawā* (desire) by bringing under control whatever the *nafs* desires at any moment. These variant terms - struggle, striving and opposition are indicators of the rigorous approach that must be undertaken to work tirelessly against the dictates of the *nafs*. Conversely, the outcome of *mujāhada* may be illusory: the seeker or aspirant may become complacent on account of the progress he makes and the virtues he gains as well as any praise he may receive from people. This attitude is prompted by the *nafs* and needs to be vigorously brought under control. The trigger of alertness as the Shaykh rightly points out is called *murāqaba* (vigilant awareness). This means that the seeker must be constantly aware that one is being watched by Allah and should, therefore, not do anything that displeases Allah. Moreover, *murāqaba* should be a lived experience rather than a spontaneous response to any situation requiring introspection of one's spiritual progress.

In line with these prerequisites, the Shaykh brings our attention to the scope and function of *ma'rifah*. This involves a certain understanding of Allah that He keeps to his promises whether to punish or reward and that His knowledge extends to one's inner thoughts, feelings, secrets, wishes and intentions.

Once the seeker develops a proper understanding and internalises it, then he can experience the reality of all this as a proof of *ma'rifah*. The Shaykh broadens the meaning of this term by stating that *mujāhada* against the devil (*shaytān*) requires a strong connection with Allah through *du'ā*. Without Allah's protection the potential danger of the situation may not be realised and inevitably may lead the seeker astray. The Shaykh adds another facet to *ma'rifah*: negative traits like pride and arrogance are stumbling blocks and must be eschewed at all times. Otherwise, the shortcomings in a seeker's moral character may not be easily recognised. Finally, the level of sincerity is accrued when the actions are done solely for the pleasure of Allah. It is built on the belief that Allah has commanded the seeker to perform certain actions, and likewise, forbidden him to partake in others. In sum, sincerity is not acquired easily, but is a gift from Allah for which *du'ā* is essential.[7]

Tawakkul

"The reality of *tawakkul* is handing over all one's affairs to Allah and moving away from the world of personal choice and personal management... and moving into the world of divine decree (*ahkām)* and ordainment (*taqdir*)."[8] The Shaykh refers to the three stages that a seeker has to undergo to have a full understanding of *tawakkul*. Essentially, the seeker must have total reliance on the promise (*wa'ā*) which Allah makes about rewards and punishments. In other words, Allah's promise is

---

[7] For a detailed discussion on *mujdhada*, see *Futuh al-Ghaib*, "Seventy-seventh Discourse," 160-62.
[8] Malik, *The Grey Falcon*, 180.

absolute; man's understanding is finite. The second stage is called *taslim* in which a seeker relies on Allah's knowledge. It entails a surrender to the will of Allah. The final stage - the highest stage is called *tafwid* or delegation. A seeker is content to accept Allah's judgement in his affairs in total submission, whether there are some worldly benefits or if he is deprived of them. However, the Shaykh makes a qualified statement for people who sidestep these stages and are under the illusion that earning a living is an impediment to their spiritual journey. The external causes (*asbāb*) of earning a living are clearly stated in the *shari'ah* through the material means of acquisition (*kasā*).

The person in his inner being (*bātin*) and heart must have an unwavering trust in Allah that whatever He has decreed after the external means will be allotted to him. This is the highest stage of *tawakkul*. Finally, these are developmental stages for a seeker in his pursuit of gaining the pleasure of Allah.

Husn al-Khuluq

There are two traits that make up *husn al-khuluq*: good character and morally virtuous behaviour. The Shaykh reminds us that in the Qur'an the Holy Prophet's (pbuh) character is expressed in these words: "And you are indeed of an exalted character."[9] Furthermore, the Shaykh states that the Holy Prophet (pbuh) was not praised for any miracle performed by him, but for his good character. The starting point of instilling a good character consists in obeying Allah's commands and staying away from what He has prohibited. A closer study of the Shaykh's approach shows his adherence to the *Sunnah*. His

---

[9] 68: 4.

elaboration of *husn al-khuluq* is not an arbitrary matter that connects the seeker with the higher realms of *tasawwuf.* For him there exists a hierarchy for the seeker to ultimately reach the goal of connecting with Allah. Too often there is a mistaken belief that spiritual bonding is an easy matter and by a quirk of fate can enable a seeker to experience the reality of *husn al-khuluq.*[10]

Shukr

Two levels of *shukr* (gratitude) form the basis of a seeker's relationship with people and with Allah. When one receives a gift from someone, he expresses his deepest appreciation for the thought and uses it for the purpose intended. As a token of appreciation, he reminds the benefactor for his gracious kindness and how the gift is of benefit to him. Likewise, thanking Allah profusely in relation to Allah's gifts and being obedient to His commands at all times is also a state of *shukr.*[11] The Shaykh was once asked to define thankfulness. He replied: "The true nature of thankfulness is the acknowledgement of the gift *(ni'mat)* of Allah, the Benefactor with an attitude of humility, a public recognition of the blessing, and a confession of one's inability to give the thanks that are due to Allah."[12] Appreciation rooted in a sense of reverence and humility characterises the highest level of *shukr.* The harmonious balance that the Shaykh advocates is aptly brought out in the concluding lines of his inspiring discourses: "Our Lord, grant us good in this world and in the Afterlife..."

---

[10] See Al-Qushayri, *Principles of Sufism,* 240-7 on the importance of *husn al- khuluq* to the enhancement of the spiritual culture.
[11] *Qaldā'id al-Jawāhir,* 572-9.
[12] *Ibid.,* 311.

Sabr

The Shaykh explains the three levels that a seeker experiences in his pursuit of spiritual excellence. Patience (*sabr*) has different dimensions in relation to Allah: first, patience for Allah implies that a seeker is patient in obeying His commands and prohibitions. Second, patience with Allah involves an accepting and conscious patience with what Allah has decreed for him in the form of trials, tribulations, sickness and bad experiences. Third, patience in Allah is the state of patience in waiting to receive whatever Allah has promised him, whether it be sustenance, success or admittance to Paradise. The Shaykh has given a nuanced understanding of the term *sabr* by using three different propositions. He quotes a *hadith* to the effect that a person cannot advance through his actions (*a'māl*) but undergoing trials and tribulations that affect his body and limbs.[13] Such a patience is reminiscent of the excruciating pain of Prophet Ayyub (A.S.) and his submission to Allah's will.[14]

Patience, according to the Shaykh, is a source of good and security in both worlds. For the seeker, it prepares him to advance from a state of equilibrium to *fanā* (annihilation). All in all, the seeker expresses patience in equal measure to circumstances that are either a source of blessing or a state of tribulation.

---

[13] *Ibid.*, 580-4.

[14] And remember when Ayyub cried to His Lord: "I have been touched with adversity, and You are the Most Merciful of the merciful." (21: 84).

Ridā

Ridā is the sense of contentment in all circumstances. Blessings or tribulations (*masā'ib*) are from Allah, requiring a believer to exercise an extreme degree of patience. Contentment also means that whatever decision Allah takes is in his best interest. Divine decree (*qadr*) according to the Shaykh is the strengthening of one's conviction (*yaqin*) that Allah's wisdom supersedes man's limited judgement and reasoning ability. By the same token, an ambivalent attitude toward *ridd* is likely to produce anxiety and wayward behaviour which is unhealthy for a seeker's well- being. The Shaykh urges the person to make an effort to make the most of one's situation and what is destined for someone will ultimately reach him. Therefore, fretting over one's circumstances, materially or otherwise, has no bearing on *ridd*, which means being satisfied with one's position and state.[15]

Sidq

The Shaykh accords the highest rank to *sidq* after prophethood. Linguistically, this term is the intensive form of truthfulness and, therefore, describes a state in which the *siddiq* is completely truthful in both deeds and actions. Another distinguishing feature of the *siddiq* is that he has forsaken all of his sins, major and minor, and does not succumb to desires (*shahawāt*) nor does he indulge in things that are considered permissible in the *shari'ah*. Furthermore, his *tawakkul is* so great that he receives his sustenance from sources he cannot imagine. In the Shaykh's view a *siddiq's* love for Allah is the only real love that is not influenced by the vagaries of time and

---

[15] *Ibid.*, 585-94.

situations. It is constant and built on faith and direct perception (*ma'rifah*). Divine decree is embraced by him and his resolve to strengthen his love for Allah intensifies in his quest to earn Allah's pleasure at all times.[16]

In our study of the Shaykh's teachings the focus is on his discourses and their transformative effect on the people who attended his assemblies. The throng of people included scholars, noted sufis, aspirants (*murīds*) and listeners. Quite often there were Christians, Jews and people of other faith groups who were overwhelmed by the charisma and spirituality exuded by the Shaykh in these assemblies. And there were others who were deeply immersed in the Shaykh's exposition of the spiritual path for which a teacher (*murshid*) was required. The states (*ahwāl*) and stations (*maqāmāt*) to which the Shaykh describes in his writings are essentially a step-by-step guide for an aspirant to reach the levels of sainthood (*wilāya*). This brief comment is meant to stimulate further reading under a mentor.[17]

In practice the Shaykh charted the pathway (*tariqah*) of *tasawwuf* for the benefit of the aspirants. Three impressions by noted contemporaries of the Shaykh are a synopsis of his spiritual path. First, the Shaykh emphasised the harmonious balance between the outer *(zāhir)* and inner (*bātin*) and detachment of the lower self (*nafs*) from the worldly distractions. Second, the Shaykh focused on the synergy between word and deed; the importance of sincerity (*ikhlās*) and submissive resignation (*taslim*) in the light of the Qur'an and the *Sunnah*. Third, the Shaykh's presentation is

---

[16] *Ibid.,* 597–600.

[17] For an overview of the *tasawwuf* terms employed by the Shaykh, *Al-Fath ar-Rabbāni* is an indispensable guide. See "Fifty-fifth Discourse" which deals with some aspects of the *maqāmāt*.

emblematic of his connection with Allah for which he was raised in rank and position which few *awliyā* enjoyed.[18]

---

[18] *Qalā'id al-Jawāhir*, 86-7.

CHAPTER NINE

Noble Character of the Shaykh

A biographical sketch of the Shaykh has to be reconstructed from the details found in his works. Although these are not comprehensive in scope, they are at least a synopsis of the illustrious personality of the Shaykh. It should be remembered that there is no chronological presentation of his life and times except from the scattered accounts of the earlier biographies and the discourses which were delivered on particular dates. In the same vein, there is an overlapping of stories and anecdotes that points out to his major contributions to the *islāh* and *tajdid* tradition.

A question arises: What were the singular qualities of the Shaykh that brought him immortal fame.? He is known by titles that are uniquely associated to his larger-than-life personality; however, there are other aspects that make him a model worth emulating. An overall impression by Imām Abu 'Abdullah al-Ishbili describes the versatility of the Shaykh in these words:

> The Shaykh was one of the supporting pillars of Islam, and the source of benefit to both the elite and the ordinary people. He was someone whose prayer was sure to be answered, readily moved to tears, constant in the practice of remembrance (*dhikr*), frequently engaged in contemplation, tender-hearted, always of good cheer, kindly by disposition, generous of hand, remarkable for knowledge, noble in traits of character, and noble by lines of descent, as well as having a firm foothold in worshipful service (*'ibādah*) and the exercise of independent

judgement (*ijtihād*).[1]

Shaykh Tosun Bayrak gives a poignant description of the Shaykhs' personality:

> The Shaykh had a soft heart, a gentle nature and a smiling face. He was sensitive and possessed the best of manners. He was aristocratic in character, generous and giving both of material things and of advice and knowledge. He loved people, but especially those who were believers and served and worshipped the One Whom they believed.
>
> The Shaykh was handsome and well-dressed. He did not speak excessively, but when he did speak, though he spoke fast, every single word and syllable was clear. He spoke beautifully and he spoke the truth. He spoke the truth without fear, for he did not care whether he was praised or criticised and condemned.[2]

Across the spectrum of the Shaykh's interaction with scholars of different backgrounds, the Mufti of Iraq, Muhyi al-din al-Baghdadi provides a vivid description of the former's character. The Shaykh was quick to shed tears, and intensely overwhelmed by the fear (*khawf*) of Allah. His entire disposition was illumined with reverence. He was honourable in his traits of character (*akhlāq*) and was the furthest from people of immoral behaviour. His discourses were filled with the theme of truth (*haqq*) and this explains why he was extremely stern in his response to those who transgressed the laws of the *shari'ah*.

---

[1] *Qalā'id al-Jawāhir*, 27.
[2] *Sirr al-Asrār*, xxi.

He was never angry with anyone and never supported any cause other than his Lord. He never turned a beggar away empty handed even if it meant if he had to give away one of his only pair of shirts. He was ready to help those in need at all times. Like a true scholar-sufi, the Shaykh was imbued with extensive knowledge *('ilm)* which was translated into practice and brought him closer to Allah through *ma'rifah* (direct experience). Truthfulness, openness and tolerance were the hallmarks of his character. In sum, he embodied the dictates of the *shari'ah* in his personal life and embedded the true content of *haqiqah* (reality as the highest stage in *tasawwuf*).[3]

In his discourses we find the Shaykh's attitude toward material possessions as inconsequential when compared to his vision of *islāh* of the community. The accounts by Jubba'i underscore the Shaykh's indifference to personal gifts, tokens of appreciation and royal presents in honour of his towering spiritual aura. When someone brought the Shaykh some gold, he would instruct his special attendant *(khādim)* to put it under the prayer rug *(sajjāda)* and the tell his servant to give it to the baker and grocer. Whenever a robe of honour was given by the Caliph he would give to the miller. He would then accept some flour from him as a loan for the sake of the needy, destitute and his guests. Rich merchants would approach the Shaykh for the disbursement of the goods as *zakāh*, ostensibly in a show of piety. The Shaykh's response was direct and forceful: "Just give them away - not only those who deserve them, but also those who do not deserve them."[4] Allah had granted the Shaykh *firāsat* (intuitive insight) to read their thoughts and motives.

The famous maxim of the Shaykh demonstrated his

---

[3] *Qalā'id al-Jawāhir*, 83-4.
[4] *Ibid.*, 149-50.

unwavering love and affection for the poor, needy and destitute: "People hanker after positions of association with the rich and elite; who really cares about the poor and needy?"[5] This attitude further explains the Shaykh's indifferent attitude toward the Caliph of the day and the bureaucrats who exhausted all possible ways to reach out to the Shaykh. In keeping with his spirit of independence the Shaykh would exit from another door when these elites sat in his room as a mark of respect.[6]

In one of his *hajj* travels, the Shaykh proceeded to a place called *Halla* with the intention to stay overnight there. He enquired from a resident if there were people in financial straits. The residents pointed to a large family living in a mud baked house. It was in a dilapidated condition with blankets separating the rooms. The Shaykh sought permission from the elderly father if he could stay with them which he readily agreed. Word spread around the village of the Shaykh's presence and it was not long when a committee approached the Shaykh to grace his presence at their homes, too. They offered him valuable items, livestock and cash which the Shaykh politely declined. Instead, he told them to give these to the poor family. The next day the Shaykh left for Makkah. 'Abdur Razzāq, the esteemed son of the Shaykh reported that many years later when he visited the family in *Halla* what he witnessed was truly amazing. The family were leading a prosperous life with an abundance of livestock and was counted among the wealthy families of the village. This was the blessing (*barakah*) of that single night and expressive of the Shaykh's sincere love for the poor and destitute.[7]

The Shaykh was the embodiment of truthfulness (*sidq*) which was evident in his first encounter with the highway robbers

---

[5] *Faruqi, Seerat-e-Ghaws-e-'Azam*, 194.
[6] *Ibid.*, 193.
[7] *Ibid.*, 198-9.

while on his way to Baghdad in pursuit of higher Islamic education. For the Shaykh truthfulness was non-negotiable and this explains his harsh criticism against those who thrived on lies, deceit and hypocrisy. In contrast, a sense of goodness (*khayr*) defines one's character and makes one a productive Muslim both in character and deed. The Shaykh related his early childhood experience about the nature of goodness: "When I was just a little boy, I used to go off by myself to spend time alone in isolated spaces. At certain moments, I would hear a voice, although I never saw a person, saying:' 'You are surely blessed with goodness, and you will surely acquire goodness!' Whenever this would happen, I would get up and explore my surroundings, since I had no idea where that voice might be coming from – for which all praise is due to Allah – I have experienced blessed grace (*barakah*) in all circumstances."[8]

The Shaykh makes a poignant remark about the importance of being blessed in the company of the *awliyā* as was the case of his moral training by Shaykh Mukharrimi and Shaykh al-Dabbās. Grounding of good character and assimilating the virtues of the friends of Allah are essential in developing a true sense of *taqwā*. The Shaykh elaborates:

> This man is a saintly friend of Allah (Almighty and Glorious is He), protected within Allah's veil, possessing safety and plenty of intelligence, a companion of the All-Merciful, blessed with His favour. Goodness - all that is good-is with him. It therefore behoves you to befriend him, to associate with him, to serve him, to endear yourself to him by taking care of things he may happen to need, and by providing him with the facilities he can

---

[8] *Jalā' al-Khawātir*, 227-8.

use. Then Allah will love you and choose you, and include you in the company of His friends and righteous servants, through His grace, if Allah wills.[9]

Mention has been made about the effect the Shaykh had on his listeners in his *majālis*. Ibn Hajar 'Asqalānī who wrote a multivolume commentary on the celebrated *hadith* collection, *Bukhāri* makes insightful comments about the Shaykh's charismatic personality in these words:

> The Shaykh used to hold a public session (*majlis*), in which he moved his audience to sighing and weeping, and in which he stirred his companions to actions. You might have supposed that the mountains were solid, but they would be floating like the clouds. There was no limit to his exercise of judgement (*ijtihād*) and his dedication to the sacred struggle (*jihād*).
>
> The Shaykh was *mukhlis* (sincerely devoted to the truth), more than any of his contemporaries, and *mukhlas* (completely untainted by hypocrisy). His trust in Allah was total and real, even though he was reminiscent of those people "who used to sleep but a little of the night." (51: 17)[10]

In a glowing tribute to the multidimensional personality of the Shaykh, Imām Nawawi (d. 1277), the exemplary scholar of *hadith* literature and commentator on the authentic *hadith* compilation, *Sahih Muslim* has expressed in eloquent terms

---

[9] *Futuh al-Ghaib*, 84.
[10] *Qalā'id al-Jawāhir*, 547-8.

the contributions of the Shaykh:

In all that has reached us, from trustworthy reporters, concerning the *karāmāt* of the saints, no one surpasses that of the *Qutb* (the axis or perfect human being), Shaykh 'Abd al-Qādir al-Jilāni. His teachings were propagated by thousands of his *murīds* many of whom reached the sublime spiritual states. The *shaykhs* and scholars were unanimous in declaring him worthy of the greatest honour and respect, in confirming his authority, in referring to his statements and referring to his judgements (*fatāwā*).

Visitors flocked to him from every corner and region... and hopes were pinned on him from every direction. Followers of the spiritual path (*ahl al-suluk*) came to him from the deepest valleys (to benefit from his discourses).

The Shaykh was handsome in his attributes, noble in his traits of character, perfectly refined in his manners and his civility (*muru'ah*), extremely humble, constantly cheerful, abundantly endowed with knowledge and intelligence, and strict in his adherence to the *shari'ah*. He treated the *'ulama* with profound respect, and honoured those who were committed to the teachings of the Qur'an and the *Sunnah*. Likewise, he hated those who were addicted to heretical innovation *(bid'ah)* and passionate desires.

The Shaykh had a sublime way of discussing the intricate points of ma'rifah. He was generous and magnanimous as far as charitable deeds (*khayrāt*) were concerned in the most beautiful way. To put it in a nutshell, there was none like him in his day and age.[11]

---

[11] *Ibid.*, 555-6. These extracts have been adapted from Imam Nawawi's *Bustān al-'Ārifīn* (Gardens of the Gnostics).

The discourses of the Shaykh brought an upsurge of religious enthusiasm among the masses. In a bustling cosmopolitan city like Baghdad – the repository of rich Islamic history and heritage – it was natural that people would be preoccupied with worldly considerations. Needless to say, the changing political fortunes of the Abbasid Caliphate and the consolidation of the Seljuq dynasty were confrontational power struggles that had a direct impact on the cohesive Islamic identity. These governments over time were suspicious of the Islamic resurgence taking place in Baghdad and beyond. Their fragile hold over power was intended to curtail the Islamic movements and erroneously perceive them as a threat to their leadership.

In these circumstances which were fraught with political instability the only alternative to rejuvenate the spirit of Islam was to create a strong consciousness among the people to commit themselves to the teachings of Islam in their daily life. Thus, people were called upon to take an oath of allegiance (*bay'ah*) for this purpose. It was actually following the footsteps of the Holy Prophet (pbuh) in the form a spiritual guide (*murshid*) who would obtain the *bay'ah* from the people to offer sincere repentance (*tawba*) and to lead a virtuous life based on the precepts of the guide. It was a spiritual journey that led the seeker or disciple (*murīd*) to be led, stage by stage, in performing the following acts: cleansing oneself of spiritual impurities; renouncing the attachment to worldly pleasures and desires; adhering to the teachings of the Qur'an and the *Sunnah*, and illumination of the soul. In this process the pledge was meant to infuse a new dynamic spirit and develop a spiritual culture compatible with the teachings and message of the primary sources of Islam.

The reformers had a broad vision of the need of the hour and used the Prophetic model as the unerring guide to establish their methodology accordingly. In the course of Islamic history millions of people have been guided to attain the stage of 'the reality of faith' (*haqiqat al-imān*) and moral and spiritual excellence (*ihsān*). Of all the mentors the Shaykh stands out as the illuminated soul who brought about a revival and resurgence unsurpassed in all times. In addition, the method he advocated still continues to hold sway over millions of people in a climate of hostility, sectarian divide and aggressive opportunism. All in all, the Qādiriyyah order as it became widely known is free from the spirituality overload and technicalities, and is a clarion call for people to be imbued with faith and enthusiasm in following the tenets of Islam.[12]

There is a general tendency to criticise the Shaykh for not setting up an Islamic state rather than spending time in delivering discourses and promoting the spiritual path. This flawed line of argument stems from a political reading of Islamic revivalism.[13] The Shaykh was fully aware that the Abbasid Caliphate were Arabs and Hashimis who traced their ancestry to the family of the Holy Prophet (pbuh). However, they could not acquit themselves befitting the position of a Caliph in Islam. The Shaykh was convinced that the root cause of their failure lay in their excessive attachment to power and wealth. In response to these rampant failures of the Caliphate, the Shaykh also undertook the bold task of saving the Islamic society from

---

[12] Fazlur Rahman Ansari, *The Qur'anic Foundations and Structure of Muslim Society.* vol.1 (Karachi, 2012), 170-2. The author gives a succinct explanation of the stages of *tasawwuf* that are in accord with the Shaykh's brilliant exposition of the inner disciplines of Islam.

[13] This mindset appears in the Islamist discourse where *tasawwuf* is either marginalised or discredited as a foreign element injected into the body politic of Islamic reformist thought.

debasement and degeneration. His sermon assemblies inspired greater awe than the Abbasid Caliphate - a testament to his powerful vision of Islamic reform. The successive waves of spiritual conquest by his children, family members, mentors and disciples in Africa, Middle East, South Asia and South East Asia are the Shaykh's lasting legacy.[14] The Turkish folk poets boast of the Shaykh's winsome personality in these elegant lines:

I am the honey of his bee, I am the rose of his garden,
I am the nightingale of his meadow
of my sheikh 'Abdu'l Qādir![15]

---

[14] Salik, *The Saint of Jilan*, 86-90.
[15] Annemarie Schimmel, *Mystical Dimensions of Islam* (North Carolina, 1975), 248.

Chapter Ten

Wasāyā (Testaments) of the Shaykh

The Shaykh had envisaged a comprehensive *islāhi* approach in promoting the teachings and message of the Qur'an and the *Sunnah* for the benefit of the *ummah*. The *wasiyya* (testament) is an important document that covers the essential guidelines for a believer to develop *taqwā* in their lives in all circumstances. In the *wasiyya* the Shaykh simplifies the overall teachings contained in his major writings; however, they are meant to be a perennial source of guidance and a beacon of hope for the *ummah* in general to re-establish their link to the Prophetic culture. We have seen the role played by the Shaykh's sons in advancing the cause of his mission – rejuvenating the Islamic consciousness among the masses in Baghdad. As successors of the legacy left behind by their illustrious father, they made sustained efforts to carry out the *islāhi* efforts which over time reached many parts of the Muslim world. As an inspirational mentor and influential figure, the Shaykh ensured that the advice and counsel for his sons would perpetuate the vision and the mission that he carried out uninterruptedly for over fifty years.

The following section contains excerpts from three advices and counsels *wasāyā* of the Shaykh. The style is simple and forceful; the message is expressive and powerful. The life-enriching lessons for the *ummah* are self-evident.

Advice and Counsel Bequeathed by the Supreme Helper (*Wasāyā Ghawthiyya*)

O my dear son! I counsel you to practise true devotion (*taqwā*) to Allah and to be ever fearful of offending Him. I also advise you to be ready at all times to fulfil your duties to your parents and your duties to all the elders (*mashā'ikh*), for Allah looks with favour upon His servant when he acts accordingly.

You must always be a faithful custodian of the Truth (*Haqq*), both in private and in public.

You must not neglect the recitation of the Qur'an, both outwardly and inwardly, in private and in public, with understanding and reflection and the shedding of tears.

Do not be one of those sufis of the ignorant and vulgar type, and shun the people of the marketplaces, for they are the thieves of our religion and the highwaymen on the road of the Muslims.

You must adhere to the beliefs of those who affirm the Divine Unity (*ahl al-tawhīd*), and steer clear of newly concocted doctrines (*mubhadathāt*), for every concocted doctrine is a heretical innovation (*bid'ah*).

Eat nothing but lawful food (*halāl*), for it is the key to all good things, and do not touch unlawful things (*harām*), unless you want the fire of Hell to touch you on the Day of Resurrection.

Be aware of Allah and do not forget your station (of humility) in the presence of Allah. Make it your frequent practice to perform the ritual prayer (*salāh*) during the night, and to fast during the daytime.

Wasāyā (Testaments) of the Shaykh

Be careful not to hurt the feelings of your elders.

Do not let compliments go to your head, and do not attach importance to critical comments that may be made about you. Let praise and blame be of matters of equal indifference as far as you are concerned.

Be on your best behaviour with your fellow men, and always adopt a humble attitude towards them.

It is important for you to cultivate good manners under all circumstances, regardless of whether you are dealing with righteous people or with immoral characters. You must accord favourable treatment to all, be they young or old, little or great. You must never regard them with anything less than a sympathetic eye.

O my dear son! Do not pay special attention to anyone until it is clearly apparent to you that he possesses these five characteristics: (1) He prefers poverty to affluence. (2) He prefers the Afterlife to this world. (3) He prefers humility to haughty pride. (4) He is keenly aware of what is done in secret and what is done in public. (5) He is prepared to face death.

O my dear son! You must accustom yourself to solitude. You must be lonely, separate, attentive to your heart because of the fear of Allah. You must acknowledge the generous favours of Allah. You must live your life in this world as if you were a stranger in exile, and then depart from it as soon as you came into it, for you have no way of knowing what tomorrow has in store for you at the Day of Resurrection (*yawm al-qiyāmat*).[1]

---

[1] The Shaykh offers this thoughtful advice: "O my people, accept the advice that I am offering you! You must detach yourself from this world, for your fondness and love for it will set up a barrier to keep you from the Afterlife, from the nearness of your Lord, and from the delight of the eyes of your hearts. Getting stuck with this world will block you off from the Afterlife, while getting stuck with the lower self (*nafs*) will block you off from the Lord of Truth." Cited in *Jalā' Al-Khawātir*, 283.

(This concludes the wise advice expressed in such noble words by Shaikh 'Abd al-Qādir).[2]

The Testament (*Wasiyya*) of the venerable 'Abd al-Qādir al-Jilāni (may Allah sanctify his innermost being)

O traveller on the path of Truth and Reality!

The advice I am bequeathing you is this: You must be fully committed to worshipful obedience *('ibādah)* and true devotion (*taqwā*). You must observe the external requirements of the *shari'ah*. You must keep your inner feeling in good health. You must be endowed with self-sacrifice, generosity combined with openness of the heart, and a smiling face. You must give without expecting anything in return. You must abstain from inflicting injury and cruelty. You must endure ill-treatment and poverty.

You must treat the eminent personalities (*mashā'ikh*) with respect, be well-behaved with your brothers in Islam, and conduct yourself with the utmost degree of benevolence in relation to the small and the great alike. Do not quarrel with other people, and do not be hostile to anyone. You must make a habit of kindness and compassion. You must refrain from accumulating wealth, unless it is by lawful means.

I advise you to preserve your personal dignity while engaging in friendship with the rich, and to be open-hearted and sincere while engaging in fellowship with the poor.

Of all human beings, the nearest to Allah is the one who is most excellent in moral character.

---

[2] *Ibid.*, 296-99.

In every situation and activity, you must remember Allah, because remembrance (*dhikr*) is all-embracing. You must cling tight to Allah's spiritual rope, because this rope is the instrument that does away with injuries (moral and spiritual) and perils (trials and tribulations).

You must obey Allah, Allah's Messenger (pbuh) and those who govern on their behalf. You must pay their rightful due, and be patient with things that are required by them. You must not attempt to press your own rightful claims immediately.

If you harbour some bad feeling towards another person, you must not stretch out on your bed. If someone does you wrong, you must pray for him with goodness and right guidance. You must recognise Allah as the only Supervisor.

You must be careful to eat lawful food. About things you do not know, you must ask those individuals who acquire knowledge for Allah's sake. In relation to Allah, you must always feel a sense of shame. Your fellowship must be with Allah. You must make a charitable donation (*sadaqah*) every morning, in keeping with your financial circumstances.[3]

The Testament (*Wasiyya*) bequeathed by the venerable 'Abd al-Qādir al-Jīlāni (may Allah sanctify his innermost being) to his son 'Abd ar-Razzāq

O my son! May Allah (Exalted is He) bestow His enabling grace upon us, and upon you and all Muslims.

First of all, I am advising you to practise true devotion to Allah, to worship him in the proper manner, and to observe the limits set by the *shari'ah*.

---

[3] *Mukhtasar fi' 'Ilm ad-Din*, 161-3.

You must know that the spiritual path (*tariqah*) of ours is founded upon the Book (Qur'ān) and the *Sunnah*, as well as the integrity of the feelings, generosity of the hand and openness of the heart. The foundation of this edifice also includes abstinence from causing injury and pain, endurance of the suffering that is to come, and the readiness to pardon our Muslim brothers for their mistakes and shortcomings at our expense. I am also advising you to be respectful toward the great leaders of Islam and the men of knowledge, to be kind to everyone great and small, not to treat anyone with hostility, except those who malign your religion, and to refrain from quarrelling and argument.

You must also know that *tasawwuf* is built on eight fine virtues, namely:

1. Liberal generosity,
2. Contentment,
3. Patience,
4. Symbolic instruction,
5. Living away from home,
6. Wearing the dervish cloak made of coarse wool (*suf*),
7. Wandering travel (in a state of abstinence) and
8. Spiritual poverty (*faqr*).[4]

You must never fail to practise sincere devotion. You must not forget that sincere devotion means forgetting about the impression you may be making on your fellow men (*khalq*),

---

[4] *Ibid.*, 166. These virtues, according to the Shaykh are synonymous with the distinctive quality of the Prophets. For example, life in exile (living from home) is the special virtue of Prophet Yusuf (A.S.) while spiritual poverty (*faqr*) is the special characteristic of the Holy Prophet (SAAS).

and paying constant attention to the view of Allah, the Creator (*Khaliq*).

You must rely on Allah, and on Him alone, in all circumstances and conditions. You must not entrust your needs to other people, on the basis of some connection between you and them, such as family ties, affection and friendship.

The most meritorious of all deeds is the preservation of the inner being from paying attention to anything other than Allah.

Spiritual poverty *(faqr)* and spiritual culture (*tasawwuf*) are two very serious matters, so you must beware of mixing them with things that are not serious.

This is my advice to you and to anyone else among the seekers who is capable of heeding it. Only Allah can enable you, and us, to explain and understand the things that I have set forth here. May Allah include us among those who follow in the footsteps of the righteous predecessors (*salaf*), in honour of our master, our Prophet and our intercessor, Muhammad (Allah bless him and give him peace). May Allah bless him, his loyal followers and his Companions (*Sahābah*), and may He grant them abundant peace, until the Day of Judgement.

Praise be to Allah, the Lord of all the Worlds.[5]

---

[5] *Ibid.*, 165-8.

CHAPTER ELEVEN

Pithy Sayings of the Shaykh

The pithy sayings of the Shaykh are gems of wisdom and advice which are couched in an elegant literary style and are a treasure trove of his decades-long teaching and preaching to countless people searching for the true essence of the Qur'an and the *Sunnah*.

There are several ways of approaching these pithy sayings from a contextual perspective. First, the Shaykh used to observe moments of silence and some illumination would inspire him to make a remark that had a direct bearing on a particular matter. Second, it was not unusual for him to make an insightful comment in the course of his discourse, perhaps a simple statement or comment that would leave his listeners in tears. Third, several questions were often posed to the Shaykh about intricate issues pertaining to *tasawwuf* and he would in the course of his explanation refer to the saying of a distinguished sufi master which mirrored his thoughts, as well. Last, the Shaykh was a spiritual guide (*murshid*) who emphasised moral training *(tarbiyyah)* for the masses as a way of transforming their lives. His charismatic presence combined with his sayings (*aqwāl*) gave depth and meaning to the Muslim community who were searching for solace amid the volatile political conditions and drift to materialism in Baghdad.

A few examples about the Shaykh's wise sayings are useful pointers to help the readers appreciate the profound effect these had on his listeners:

"The world is full of busy preoccupations and the Afterlife is full of uncertainties. The servant of the Lord is caught between these two situations, until his final destination is established, whether it will be the garden of Paradise or the fire of Hell."[1]

"A spiritual pauper (*faqir*) not to be confused with a beggar - must be dignified and very patient, content and very thankful. He must be truthful of tongue, and steadfast of heart. He should treat his guests with cordial hospitality and supply everyone present with whatever food is available."[2]

It is evident that the Shaykh draws upon the daily experiences of life to press home important messages that the listeners or audience can relate to. He also avoids the beaten path of complex concepts to elucidate the essence *of tasawwuf.* For example, the word pauper (*faqir*) is likely to conjure up an image of destitution, helplessness and despondency. In contrast, the Shaykh presents a positive image to position the important role of the *faqir* in relation to the spiritual path (*tariqah*) he follows.

"Your fellow men are the veil that screens you from your own self (*nafs*), and your own self is the veil that screens you from your Lord (*Rabb*)".[3]

The battle lines between the *nafs* and spiritual growth are clearly drawn. This theme is discussed in greater detail in the Shaykh's celebrated works.

We have selected thirty pithy sayings of the Shaykh, illustrating his perceptive insight into the temperament of people and their outlook on life:

1. "A heart that does not believe is like a cage that has no bird

---

[1] *Qalā'id al-Jawāhir,* 167.
[2] *Ibid.,* 319.
[3] *Ibid.,* 321.

inside it."

2. "So long as your heart does not support what is on your tongue, you cannot take a step toward the Lord of Truth (*Haqq*)."

3. "O my Lord! Enter the house of our heart without the slightest hesitation, because there is nothing in it whatsoever apart from the pain of separation from You."

4. "When you have committed a sin, you must not lose hope of Allah's mercy. You must use the water of repentance to wash away the dirt of sin that has been smeared upon you."

5. "The whole of your aspiration and endeavour must not be for the simple things like eating, drinking, clothing and marriage. That is because these are not the goal, but only the means by which to arrive at the goal."

6. "While eating lawful food is a radiant light, eating unlawful food is a suffocating darkness. Eating unlawful food kills the heart, whereas the lawful morsel brings the heart to life."

7. "While on the ocean of this world you must be extremely vigilant. You must be extremely sensitive, because many people are drowned and lost in the ocean."

8. "Consider the rules of your life, for then you will understand what you are worth."

9. "Our enemies are our greatest moral teachers, because they thrust our faults into our faces."

10. "You must keep your judgement clear of the mists of vain conceit."

11. "You must be such an ardent lover of truthfulness, that every statement you make assumes the quality of a solemn oath."

12. "We have been created to rely on one another. If a stone is removed from a wall, as if to demonstrate the risk of that wall's collapsing, and if one withdraws, we are left face to

face with the danger of its collapse."

13. "The remedy of poverty is not to bear grudges against the rich."

14. "You must not do anything while you are angry. Would the sail (of the boat) be hoisted in the storm?"

15. "The display of fame most often suppresses the voice of conscience."

16. "Your most real enemies are the greed, the envy and jealousy that live in your heart. They are the soldiers of the instigating self (*nafs al-ammārah*)."

17. "We have not invented courtesy in order to show off the goodness that does not exist in ourselves."

18. "Success is a letter delivered by three postmen. These are competence, endeavour and good fortune."

19. "Nothing can kill the pride of the lower self (*nafs*), but everything serves to enhance it."

20. "Those who make fun of you, those who try to get rid of you, they are the people whose applause you most often seek to obtain."

21. "Cowardice is one thing that cannot be repaired by any means."

22. "Hope is the money given on loan by happiness."

23. "A man who has no confidence in himself can accomplish nothing."

24. "The best of men is the person who is beneficial to others."

25. "Conscience is the best of the books of morality, so we must always make reference to it."

26. "The success of a human being is measured by the effort he has exerted in order to achieve that success."

27. "Trying to discover the faults of other people amounts to making no effort to deal with those in oneself."

28. "If you claim to have understood reality, you must only do so after putting that reality in your own life."

29. "Happiness does not exist in a place where there is no justice."

30. "Only great spirits experience the triumph of goodness.[4]"

---

[4] *Mukhtasar fi' Ilm ad-Din*, 173-77.

The Seven Levels or Stations of the Self (Nafs)

1. The "instigator" *(al-ammāra)*

The attributes of the instigating self are cupidity (greed, lust), ignorance, wickedness, envy and anger.

2. The "censorious" *(al-lawwāmah)*

The attributes of the censorious self are passion (wicked selfish lusts), lying and fraud, cunning, vain conceit, desire (for things that are not permitted) and coercion.

3. The "inspired" *(al-mulhamah)*

The attributes of the inspired self are humble submissiveness without expecting anything in return, repentance, patience and endurance.

4. The "tranquil" *(a!l-mutma'inna)*

The attributes of the tranquil self are satisfaction, generosity, knowledge, trust, endurance, reality, contentment, and thank- fulness.

5. The "contented" *(ar-rādiya)*

The attributes of the contented self are charismatic talents (*karāmāt*), abstinence, remembrance (*dhikr*) and ardent love.

6. The "pleasing" *(al-marāiyya)*

The attributes of the pleasing self are refinement of moral

character, gentleness, nearness (to the Lord), and adherence to the exemplary conduct of the Chosen One (*Sunnat al-Mustafā*).

7. The "sincere" *"al-samina"* or also called the "pure" *(al-sāfiya)*

The attributes of the sincere/pure self are seclusion, silence, truthfulness, helpfulness, loyalty and compliance with the commandments of Allah.[1]

---

[1] Adapted from *Pearls of the Heart*, 169-71.

Shaykh 'Abdul Qādir Al-Jilāni[1]

In the name of A!!ah, Most Gracious, Most Merciful

The Almighty Allah blessed us with love in our hearts for the great saints, including Shaykh 'Abdul Qādir al-Jilāni (r)[2] the recipient of His (Allah's divine guidance.

Success depends on following the good deeds of one's forefathers. A French author said: "graveyards are yardsticks of progress; if well kept, they are a sign of the country's progress; if neglected, they are a sign of the country's retrogression." Also, a nation that remembers the deeds of its forefathers will flourish, but a nation that forgets its forefathers will perish."

We are here to celebrate the memory of a great person, not in order to worship him, but to emulate him. On Independence Day we commemorate the good deeds of the founder of Pakistan, Muhammad Ali Jinnah (d. 1948). The Pakistani immigrants of England, and other countries, share in this celebration. Those who change the world for the better should always be remembered. We commemorate the achievement of great leaders, so why not commemorate the achievement of great Prophets. Tonight, through the *Milād al-Nabi* (the Birthday of the Prophet (pbuh), we commemorate the achievements of the greatest Prophet that ever lived.

Allah says in the Holy Qur'ān:

---

[1] The talk was delivered at an 'Urs celebration in honour of Shaykh Abdul Qadir al-Jilani, founder of the Qadiriyyah order.

[2] *Rahimahu!!ah* (May Allah have mercy on him).

You have indeed in the Messenger of Allah a beautiful pattern of conduct (33: 21).

Say: 'If you love Allah, follow me: Allah will love you and forgive you your sins; for Allah is oft-forgiving, most merciful" (3: 31).

The verse reminds us that if we truly love Allah, we should follow the moral example of Muhammad (pbuh).

I gave a lecture in English to an audience of 70 000 people at the Green Point track in Cape Town (1952).[3] I was told that it changed the people's attitude to our noble Prophet (pbuh). They see him now as a man of peace and mercy, not a man of violence and lust. He came to remove racial discrimination between black and white, Arab and non-Arab, and taught that we should only be subservient to One God. He is indeed a paragon of virtue to be emulated, not to be despised. We should also emulate those who follow him. We should follow the friends of Allah (*awliyā*), who are connected to him spiritually, through a chain (*silsilah*) that goes back to him. These saintly personalities are examples for us.

There is confusion today about what is true knowledge and who has true knowledge. A man of knowledge is not necessarily one who wears a long garb, a long beard, and has some *Mawlana* title. The Qur'ān gives us a definition of a learned person:

And so amongst men and crawling creatures and cattle, are they of various colours. Those truly fear Allah, among

---

[3] For a detailed discussion on the talk, see Abdul Kader Choughley, *Abdul Aleem Siddiqui: Man and Mission* (Springs, 2021), 200-204.

His servants, who have knowledge: for Allah is exalted in might, oft-forgiving (35: 28).

The learned fear Allah, and are the true inheritors of the Prophet (pbuh). Even the nations of the world cannot harm them. They have been illuminated by divine light, which no disbeliever can extinguish.

Fain would they extinguish Allah's light with their mouths, but Allah will not allow but that His light should be perfected, even though the unbelievers may detest (it) (9: 32).

Allah's light is complete, all-encompassing. It protects and honours all the friends of Allah, all the heirs of Muhammad (pbuh).

Muhammad (pbuh) addressed the people of Makkah and said: "I do not fear that my followers will become unbelievers, polytheists or apostates, but I fear that they will worship wealth, oppress others, and lose their love for Allah and His Prophet." Muslims have not taken heed of this warning. They are still intoxicated by wealth. Muslims of Spain became corrupted by wealth, sand this corruption spread to Syria, and it seemed destined that Shaykh 'Abdul Qādir al-Jilāni had to be sent to this region (Baghdad and beyond) to deliver people from this corruption.

I am glad to hear that some young people are translating Urdu books on Shaykh 'Abdul Qādir al-Jilāni. This is a great service, and Muslim businessmen should support these kinds of efforts. If the translations capture the spirit of the originals, they could change the attitude of Westerners towards Islam.

Since childhood Shaykh 'Abdul Qādir used to hear voices suggesting that he was no ordinary person. This 'Urs celebration is in honour of this extraordinary personality. It is good to remember him, and listen to a lecture on him, but this is not enough. More importantly, we should practise his message.

Shaykh 'Abdul Qādir was poor, and his parents could not afford to send him for higher education. He wanted to go to Baghdad for Islamic studies. Today, people want to inherit the wealth of their fathers, but not the knowledge of their Prophets. You will fight for the inheritance of your parents, but not for the inheritance of Muhammad (pbuh). What sacrifices are we making for knowledge? A newspaper notice called for donations for an Islamic college. Fifteen people promised help, but did not fulfil their promise. What value do we give to Islamic education? Today, the Imam is merely the servant of the trustees, and the *Mawlānās* are slaves of the wealthy. The rich want to rule over them, but the *musalla* (prayer mat) they sit on does not belong to them, but to the Prophet (pbuh).

The truly learned have a great status. On the Day of Judgement, they will stand at the throne of Allah, and Allah will take account of all creation. People who did good will go to Paradise, and those who did evil will go to hell. The learned will intercede on the Day of Judgement on behalf of the sinners. But what respect do we have for the learned? We have no affection for them, and we only go to them Baghdad for work. Your mother asked me to do her a favour and said: 'Give this silver to my son in Baghdad. I do not know if he has money for food."'

The man continued and said: I could not find work and I was hungry. So, I used some of the silver to buy food. I am so sorry;

I broke your mother's trust. I came here to eat this food, so you can join me, but can I eat with your permission?" Shaykh 'Abdul Qādir partook of the meal and thought: "This is from to help us in our business. But they are not trained to look after your worldly possessions by offering you *ta'widhs* (amulets). Women go to them if they are barren, and men go to them if they are guilty of some fraud and awaiting court sentences. Jalāluddin Rumi said: "A few moments with a learned scholar are better than a hundred years of worship. It can change your heart."

Shaykh 'Abdul Qādir went to Baghdad to be in the company of the learned. His mother advised him before he left: "Speak the truth at all times." One day, while travelling by caravan, he was accosted by the robbers, and they asked him if had money, and he gave it to them. They were moved by his truthfulness and embraced Islam.

Shaykh 'Abdul Qādir was a successful student in Baghdad, but he had to make many sacrifices. His mother gave him a few dirhams from her life savings. Today, we spoil our children with the best clothes, the best homes, the best luxuries. It is such an effort for us to leave the comfort of our homes just to attend a religious lecture. Shaykh 'Abdul Qādir left the distant town of Jilan to go as far as Baghdad for knowledge. There was no boarding school, and students used to study the Qur'ān during the day and could hardly afford to eat a few green leaves at night.

Shaykh 'Abdul Qādir tells us that there was a famine in Iraq for a year; no rain, no cattle, and only a few green leaves for nourishment. People became weaker by the day, and they moved from the city to a simple mosque in the jungle. Shaykh 'Abdul Qādir was hungry for seven days, and a man entered the mosque with food. Shaykh 'Abdul Qādir said to himself: "You are starved for seven days, but if you starve for more than three days, what is forbidden to you,[4] will now be permissible. So, ask the man for food." Then he spoke to his *nafs* (lower self) and said: "O dog, it is your habit to look at other people's things. Turn to Allah, the Giver of all bounties."

The man entered and offered his food to Shaykh 'Abdul Qādir, but he chastised his *nafs* and refused to eat. The man took pity on him as he was getting weak from hunger. The man asked him his name and where he came from. Upon hearing the reply, he bowed to the ground for forgiveness and said: "I am a criminal from Jilan, and I came to my mother." He took the rest of the silver and came back to the school, and bought food for the hungry students. By the evening, he had nothing left.

Once Muhammad (pbuh) led the prayer, but immediately thereafter, he left early to go home. A Companion asked why he lefts so early, and he said: "I forgot some provisions at home, and I wanted to fetch them quickly before these go to bed hungry." Today, the stomachs of Muslims are empty, but our safes are full of money. This is our character and yet we claim to be followers of Muhammad (pbuh). Let us learn a lesson from the lifestyle of Shaykh 'Abdul Qādir, especially his sacrifices for knowledge and his upright character.

Praise be to Allah, the Lord of the worlds.[5]

---

[4] Shaykh 'Abdul Qadir did not accept any *sadaqah* (charity) or alms from people.
[5] Yasien Mohamed (editor), *The Roving Ambassador of Peace: The Lectures of Moulana Abdul Aleem Siddiqui in South Africa* (Cape Town, 2006), 41-6.

Bibliography

Al-Qushayri, Abul Qasim. *Principles of Sufism* (Berkely, 1992). *Latā'if al- Ishārāt: Subtle Illusions.* Translated by Kristin Zahra Sands (Louisville, 2017)

Al-Jilāni, Shaikh 'Abd Al-Qādir, *Al-Ghunya li Tālibi Tariq al-Haqq: Sufficient Provision for Seekers of the Path of Truth* (Florida, 1997).

Al-Fath ar-Rabbāni: The Sublime Revelation (Florida, 1992).

Futuh al-Ghaib: Revelations of the Unseen (Kuala Lumpur, 1995).

Khamsata 'Ashara Maktubān: Fifteen Letters (Florida, 1997).

Mukhtasar fi 'Ilm ad-Dīn: The Summary of Religious Knowledge and Pearls of the Heart (Florida, 2010).

Jalā Al-Khawātir: The Removal of Cares (Florida, 1997).

Malfuzāt: Utterances (Florida, 1992).

Sirr Al-Asrār: The Secret of Secrets (Cambridge, 1992).

Tafsir Jilāni (n.d.)

Al-'Asqalānī, Hāfiz ibn Hajar. *Ghibta al-Nazir fi Tarjumat al-Shaykh Abd al-Qādir* (Beirut, 1996).

Al-Hanbali, Ibn Rajab. *Al-Dhayl 'ala Tabaqāt al-Hanābila* (Riyadh, 2005).

Ali, Syed Amir. *A Short History of the Saracens* (New Delhi, 1981). Al-Musleh, Abu Bakr. *Al-Ghazāli: The Islamic Reformer* (Kuala Lumpur, 2012).

Al-Shattanawfi, 'Ali ibn Yusuf. *Bahjat al-Asrār* (Beirut, 1999).

Al-Tabari, Ibn Jarir. *The Commentary on the Qur'ān.* vol. 1. Translated by J. Cooper (Oxford, 1990).

Al-Tafidi, Muhammad ibn Yahya. *Qalā'id al-Jawāhir* (Beirut,

2005).

Ansari, Muhammad Fazlur Rahman. *The Qur'anic Foundations and Structure of Muslim Society.* vol. 1 (Karachi, 2012).

Attar Fariduddin. *Tadhkirat al-Awliyā* (Lahore, n.d.).

Bhat, Manzoor Ahmad. *Sufi Thought of Shaikh Saiyyid 'Abdu'l Qādir Jilāni and its Impact on the Indian Subcontinent* (New Delhi, 2010).

Choughley, Abdul Kader (editor). *Moral and Spiritual Transformation in Islam* (Springs, 2019).

Abdul Aleem Siddiqui: Man and Mission (Springs, 2021).

Fazlur Rahman Ansari: Life and Thought (Springs, 2012).

Dhahabi, Shamsuddin. *Sayr A'lāmal-Nubalā.* Translated by D.S. Margoliouth. *Contributions to the Biography of 'Abd Al-Kādir of Jilān*, JRAS (1907).

Faruqi, Muhammad Dawud. *Sirat i-Ghaws e-'Azam* (Amritsar, 1926).

Gailani, Noorah. *The Shrine of 'Abd al-Qādir al-Jilāni* (2016).

Ibn Kathīr, 'Umar. *Al-Bidāya wa al-Hidāya* (Beirut, 1988).

Ibn Rajab, Ahmad. *Tabaqāt al-Hanābila* (Beirut, 1980).

Jullundhri, Rashid Ahmad. *Qur'anic Exegesis in Classical Literature with particular Reference to Abul al-Qāsim al-Qushayri* (Kuala Lumpur, 2010).

Malik, Hamza. *The Grey Falcon: Life and Teaching of Shaykh 'Abd a!- Qādir al-Jilāni* (Leiden, 2018).

Mohamed, Yasien. *The Roving Ambassador of Peace: The Lectures of Moulana Abdu Aleem Siddiqui in South Africa* (Cape Town, 2006).

Nadwi, Abul Hasan Ali. *Saviours of the Islamic Spirit.* vol.1 (London, 2015).

Nasr, Jamil Abun. *Muslim Communities of Grace* (London

2007). Nasr, Seyyed Hossein. *Islamic Spirituality: Manifestations* (New York, 1991).

Qadri, Muhammad Riaz. *The Sultan of the Saints: Mystical Life and Teachings of Hazrat Shaikh Syed Abdul Qadir Jilani* (New Delhi, 2020).

Qari, Mulla 'Ali, *Nuzhat al-Khawātir al-Fātir* (Lahore, 2003).

Salik, Saiyed Abdus. *The Saint of Jilan* (Calcutta, 1939).

Sands, Kristin Zahra, *Sufi Commentaries on the Qur'ān in Classical Islam* (New York, 2006).

Schimmel, Annemarie. *Mystical Dimensions of Islam* (North Carolina, 1975).

Sharif, M.M. *A History of Muslim Philosophy.* vol. 1 (Karachi, 1983).

Suhrawardi, Shihabuddin. *Awārif al-Ma-'arif* (New Delhi, 1981).

Trimingham, Spencer. *The Sufi Orders in Islam* (Oxford, 1998).